A MONEY FOR YOUR MONEY GUIDE

Free Stuff for Your Pet

Linda Bowman

PROBUS PUBLISHING COMPANY
Chicago, Illinois

This publication is designed to provide accurate and authoritative, information in regard to the subject matter covered. It is sold with the understanding that the publisher is not engaged in rendering legal, accounting or other professional service. If legal or other expert assistance is required, the services of a competent professional should be sought.

ISBN 1-55738-271-9

Printed in the United States of America

IPC

1   2   3   4   5   6   7   8   9   0

Illustrations © Carol Lea Benjamin, cover, pp. 5, 30, 47, 66, 86, 113, 128

Typeset and design by Carol Barnstable

CONTENTS

DEDICATION

A DOG'S PLEA

Treat me kindly, my beloved friend, for no heart in all the world is more grateful for kindness than my loving heart.

Do not break my spirit with a stick, for though I might lick your hand between blows, your patience and understanding will more quickly teach me the things you would have me learn.

Speak to me often, for your voice is the world's sweetest music as you must surely know by the fierce wagging of my tail when the sound of your footstep falls upon my waiting ear.

Please take me inside when it is cold and wet, for I am a domesticated animal, no longer accustomed to bitter elements. I ask no greater glory than the privilege of sitting at your feet beside the hearth.

Keep my pan filled with fresh water, for I cannot tell you when I suffer thirst.

Feed me clean food so I may stay well, to romp and play and do your bidding, to walk by your side and stand ready, willing and able to protect you with my life, should your life be in danger.

And, my friend, when I am very old and I no longer enjoy good health, hearing and sight, do not make heroic efforts to keep me going. I am not having any fun. Please see to it that my life is taken gently. I shall leave this earth knowing with the last breath I draw that my fate was always safest in your hands.

— Anonymous

BEFORE YOU GET STARTED . . .

Many of the items in this book are yours for free. If an item is noted as FREE, the most you will pay is the postage for sending a postcard or letter. In many cases you can call a toll-free number to receive the item or information—even better since it costs you absolutely nothing! Be sure to check and see if the company you are contacting has a toll-free number before sending them a letter.

If they don't have a toll-free number you must mail your request either by sending in a letter or postcard. Send a letter if the company requests a SASE (self-addressed stamped envelope) or a small fee (usually between 50¢ - $2) to offset postage and handling costs. When sending a SASE, make sure that the envelope is business size (referred to as #10 and measuring 9" long and 4" wide). Clearly address the envelope to yourself, place a first class stamp on it, fold it and insert it in an envelope addressed to the company you are writing to.

If the company only needs your name and address in order to send you a FREE item, send a 19¢ postcard and save yourself 10¢ postage. Again, make sure your name, address and zip code is clearly printed on the back of the postcard.

Always specify the exact item you want. Use the name of the item or title (if it's a publication) just as you find it in this book. Since some companies have several offers or publish several different booklets, they might not know exactly what you want unless you clearly tell them. It usually takes six to eight weeks for your request to be processed and the item sent to you.

Finally, although we have made our best efforts to insure that all the information and offers described in the book are valid, we cannot guarantee they will still be available at the time you request them. Since companies may have only a limited stock on hand of a particular item, booklet or sample, it is possible it may not be available. You might want to request a current list of free publications or other information as most companies are constantly updating and coming out with new offers which supercede their previous ones.

CHAPTER 1

The love for all living creatures
is the most noble attribute
of man.

-- Charles Darwin

THE FAMILY PET

 People just love their family pets. We play with them, ride them, cuddle with them, watch them, travel with them, train them, grow up with them, grow old with them, exercise with them, depend on them, talk to them and scold them. They are truly cherished members of our family.

Not unlike children, their care and feeding can become an expensive investment over the long run. Veterinary bills, food and vitamin bills, bills for toys and treats, supplies (bedding, blankets, shampoos, conditioners, collars, bridles, shoes, saddles, collars, cages and so on) all add up. The list of what we spend on our pets seems neverending. A recent survey has shown that in the 1990s pet-related spending (i.e. veterinary care, pet services and pet food) will increase by as much as 30 percent, totaling more than $12 billion. Dollars spent on pet services are expected to climb more than 50 percent, from $960 million to over $1.4 billion. Expenditures on pet food will increase from $5.5 billion to more than $7 billion by the year 2000. Some pet food industry experts estimate the amount spent is even higher, nearing the $8 billion mark.

More than ever, the pet marketplace is flooded with an endless stream of products. For example, there are more than 90 brands of cat food available in the U.S. today. Whether we own fancy gold fish or Kentucky Fox Trotters, most of us would like to give our pets the "best that money can buy," but not all of us can afford to. In the blink of an eye, pet owners can easily spend hundreds and often thousands of dollars a year taking care of their furry, feathered, four-legged and waterbound friends.

As a pet owner (three dogs, one cat, thirteen koi and two horses) I have always looked for savings in pet shops, feed stores and magazines advertisements. What I discovered is that there is a tremendous array of little known FREE and low cost products and services available for our domestic friends. The trick is to know where and how to find these great discounts and savings. Even if raising children in today's world costs "an arm and a leg," raising and caring for our animals doesn't have to.

This book will provide you with the information you need to take advantage of incredible FREE services and products for pets. I also have included information that will guarantee you substantial savings when a freebie just isn't possible. Whether you have cats, dogs, fish, birds or horses, you can begin enjoying your animals even more with the bargains contained in this book. In addition, I have included sources for savings on things for pet lovers and pet owners too. Jewelry, clothing, doormats, stickers, stamps, calendars, mugs and hats emblazoned with your favorite breed are just some of the thousands of goodies and gifts available to animal lovers.

We will start with the basic issue of where and how you can get a pet, often a purebred or pedigree, for absolutely FREE. You may not be aware of the many sources of locating fine, loving animals in need of a good home. Once you have brought your new pet home, you will want to give him the best possible care to insure its health, happiness and well being.

You don't have to go back to school or take courses to learn how to care for your animals. Everything you've ever wanted to know about the care, feeding and health of your pet(s) can be easily learned from the sources that I refer you to in this book. There are hundreds of FREE pamphlets, books, articles and publications produced by manufacturers of pet products, animal protection associations, organizations and practitioners in the fields of animal health services. In fact, there is so much FREE information out there that, in many cases, you can solve your pet's problems and *save* on expensive veterinary bills by referring to these excellent, informative sources before spending your money unnecessarily.

Of course, some professionally administered medical treatments must be given to insure your pet's ongoing health and immunity against common diseases. These preventive measures are not only important for your pets (and required by law), but they also protect owners from contracting diseases transmittable between humans and animals. These vaccines and treatments can add up to a lot of money; however, there are ways of saving on these costs and sometimes even getting these services for FREE—if you know how.

Some pets are finiky eaters. Others will gobble up anything you put in front of them and ask for more. Different kinds of animals require different kinds of diets and nutritional consider-

c. benjamin

ations. A professional show dog or cat may require a different diet than a family pet. A competing Hunter-Jumper or Cross-Country horse may need supplements and vitamins not necessary for an average trail horse. Today, most animal professionals agree that pet food should be selected depending upon the pet's age and health (puppy/kitten, adult/maintenance, older/less active/mature, overweight/underweight). How can you find out what kind of diet is best for your animal(s)? By trying different foods and food combinations. Most pet food manufacturers are more than happy to provide you with FREE samples of their products. In fact, there is no reason you should spend your dollars just to try their products. Pet stores, veterinary offices and pet shows abound with FREE samples of the latest, most nutritionally advanced formulas.

Another way to save money is by clipping coupons from your daily Saturday or Sunday newspaper coupon section. Because of the fierce competition between major supermarket brand pet foods, high value (and FREE) coupon offers have become a common method for luring new customers. Since most supermarkets double manufacturers coupons, these 50¢ to $1.50 coupons can add up to great savings at the checkout counter, whether you're testing new brands or buying your regular pet food. Even "gourmet" pet food producers have gotten into the coupon act by advertising discounts and savings in pet magazines and newsletters.

You will also find great savings in many other pet services. Pet grooming, flea control, pet-sitting, training, boarding facilities and pet insurance are important services many of us need at one time or another. The more you know about these services, the more you can save when you choose which one(s) are best suited for you and your pet.

Are you interested in learning or doing more for the pet and animal community in your area? There are dozens of worthwhile organizations whose purposes are to protect and support the animal population of this country. I will talk about some of these important and interesting organizations whose continuing efforts are enhancing the quality of life for our pets and animals.

The more you know and learn about your pets, the better a "pet parent" you will be for them. To help you achieve this goal, I have included a variety of animal magazines, newsletters, books and book publishers. In most cases, I will show you how to get free sample issues and discounts on these valuable publications.

One of the best ways to compare and save on products for your pets is by shopping from mail-order catalogs. There are literally hundreds of catalogs with thousands of items for pets and pet lovers. Most of these catalogs are available FREE and many offer items at substantial savings. Why not do your comparison shopping from the comfort of your home? Your research will pay off handsomely in the dollars you'll save by finding the lowest prices and best values.

FREE STUFF FOR YOUR PETS is all around. Great savings on quality products and services are there for the asking. By becoming a smart shopper and using the information in the following chapters, you can enjoy many years with happy, healthy pets in your home and extra cash in your pocket.

CHAPTER 2

The greatness of a nation and
its moral progress can be judged
by the way its animals
are treated.

---Mohandas Karamchand Gandhi

HOW TO GET A PET FOR FREE

PUBLIC PET SHELTERS AND POUNDS

Adopting a pet through city or county departments of Animal Regulation or Animal Care and Control shelters is an easy, economical way to bring a pet into your home. Unwanted, lost, stray and abandoned animals of every shape, size, age and breed can be found at your local shelter waiting for a good home. More than 15 million pets end up in animal shelters each year and nearly 11 million of those are "put to sleep." About 30 percent of these animals are "purebreds," the majority coming from what are commonly referred to as "backyard breeders" and the "Midwest puppy mills," found in Kansas, Iowa, Missouri, Arkansas, Nebraska, Oklahoma and Pennsylvania.

These public shelters can't possibly place all the animals that are found or brought to them. Even privately funded shelters, such as local Humane Societies or SPCAs (Society for the Prevention of Cruelty to Animals), have a difficult time finding homes and human companionship for their rescued, unwanted animals. For example, a typical Humane Society shelter in Long Beach, CA houses as many as 18,000 pets a year, but, on an average, can only find homes for 1,200 of them. The animals are

How to Get a Pet for Free   11

free. Vaccinations, licenses (dogs only), medical exams, neutering or spaying, generally cost less than $35 for cats and $50 for dogs. In many cases, shelters offer FREE or low-cost services, collars and leashes to qualifying senior citizens or people with low incomes. To help you select a puppy or dog from one of these groups, you may want to pick up a copy of *The Chosen Puppy* or *Secondhand Dog* by Carol Lea Benjamin (generally available at your local humane or anti-cruelty society).

NON-PROFIT ADOPTION AGENCIES AND RESCUE GROUPS

There are many organizations that rescue animals from shelters and care for them. These groups will provide animals for FREE to qualified homes. Some of these groups specialize in rescuing specific breeds, such as Akitas, Dobermans, Terriers, Alaskan Malamutes, Basset Hounds, Welsh Corgis, Scotties, Great Pyrenees, German Shepherds, etc. Often these purebreds are older or abused animals. Many come from puppy mills and ended up sick or abandoned with problems making them unsuitable for pet stores to sell. There are also many wonderful, healthy, happy purebreds who have ended up in shelters for a variety of reasons and that make excellent companions.

Senior dogs and cats make wonderful friends for children and older adults. Some animal rescue organizations specialize in these kinds of pets, placing them in appropriate homes for free. Studies have shown that elderly people who own pets benefit both psychologically and physically from having a pet companion. The theory behind this is that pets provide comfort and companionship that older people might otherwise seek from physicians.

Retired greyhound dogs make excellent, loving pets. Three organizations which provide adoption services for retired racers are: Racers Recycled, P.O. Box 270107, Houston, TX 77277, (713)665-3366; Retired Greyhounds as Pets, P.O. Box 111,

Camby, IN 46113, (317)290-5292; and Greyhound Pets of America, (800)366-1472 . These volunteer organizations rescue hundreds of former racing greyhounds from tracks around the country. At present there are 54 Greyhound race tracks in the U.S. and the number is growing. Many tracks also offer retired racers for adoption. If you live near a track or are planning a vacation near one, ask whether they have an adoption program.

There are several ways to find out about rescue and adoption organizations. One is by checking with local veterinary clinics and pet stores (the ones that don't sell their own pets). They usually carry flyers or cards for these groups. You can find listings for city and county animal shelters in the government listing pages of your phone directory.

There are also publications devoted to publicizing animals for adoption. One such publication is *Muttmatchers Messenger,* a monthly newspaper/referral service for dogs that has several editions, covering the entire West Coast from Alaska to Mexico. *Muttmatchers* advertises hundreds of adoptable pets from both private parties and a variety of privately sponsored pet rescue groups. Examples of rescue shelters offering dogs for adoption include Friends for Pets Foundation, Little Dog Adoption, Animal Alliance, Pet Orphans Fund, Lifeline for Pets, Humane Animal Rescue Team, Foundation for Indigent Animals, Neighborhood Adoption Group, Animal Alliance and Friends of Animals Foundation. Look for animal rescue newsletters and information on shelters in your pet store or write one of the organizations listed in Chapter 9 for a shelter in your area. Also, write *Project BREED* (Breed Rescue Efforts and Education Directory) for a complete listing of organizations that provide rescue services by breed at 18707 Curry Powder Lane, Germantown, MD 20874.

In addition to rescuing pets from public animal shelters, many of the privately supported animal programs (and some humane societies) take in pets whose owners, for a variety of circumstances, are no longer able to care for them. These no-kill shelters fall into two groups: those that offer care for a pet until it is adopted, even if that care extends to the end of the animal's life; and those that offer lifetime care with a no-adoption option, a kind of "retirement home" for pets. Many of these are cageless, home-like environments where the animals live in a warm, secure, comfortable environment until adoption. The cost of adopting these animals is usually minimal, just enough to defray medical and spaying expenses. The following are examples of non-profit shelters that take in pets and care for them until they are adopted:

- Living Free Animal Sanctuary (dogs and cats), P.O. Box 5, Mountain Center, CA 92361. Contact: Bobbi Lazare.

- Cat Care Society, 5985 W. 11th Ave., Lakewood, CO 80214.

- Pet Pride's Home for Cats, P.O. Box 1055, Pacific Palisades, CA 90272.

- North Shore Animal League, 750 Port Washington Blvd., Port Washington, NY 10050.

- Helen Woodward Animal Center, 6461 El Apajo, P.O. Box 64, Rancho Santa Fe, CA 92067.

- Sido Program, 2500 16th Street, San Francisco, CA 94103.

- National Cat Protection Society, 1528 W. 17th St., Long Beach, CA 90813.

- The Bosler Humane Society, P.O. Box 520, Barre, MA 01005.

- Actors and Others for Animals, 5510 Cahuenga Blvd, No. Hollywood, CA 91601.

- American Society for the Prevention of Cruelty to Animals, 441 E. 92nd Street, New York, NY 10128.

- Bide-A-Wee Home Association, 410 E. 38th Street, New York, NY 10016.

🐐 International Defenders of Animals, Box 175, San Marin, CA 95046.

🐐 Pioneers for Animal Welfare Society, Box 861, Hicksville, NY 11802.

🐐 Orphan Alley, N2658 C.T.A., Gresham, WI 54128.

For the past two years, *Cat Fancy* magazine has published (in the August issue) an updated list of no-kill shelters offering adoption, lifetime care or retirement programs for pet owners and those seeking to adopt a pet. Check your local library or send $4.00 to *Cat Fancy*, Back Issue Dept., P.O. Box 6050, Mission Viejo, CA 92690 (request the most recent August issue).

GUIDE DOGS

If you are interested in adopting a dog, you might want to look into adopting one from one of the many guide dog centers around the country. Today there are approximately 5,000 dogs working as guide dogs for the blind and thousands more being used to help handicapped people who are deaf, quadriplegic, paraplegic or suffering from such diseases as multiple sclerosis or spina bifida. As well as being loving companions, these dogs are the eyes and ears of their handicapped owners.

It takes a great deal of training for a dog to qualify for this work. They must be at ease in all types of living conditions such as heavy traffic, loud noises, crowded pedestrian areas and with other animals. Because the standards are so high for these dogs, as many as 50 percent are often rejected from a typical guide dog program and placed in an adopted home permanently.

The benefit of having such a dog is that they are AKC registered purebreds, usually German Shepherds, Golden Retrievers and Labrador Retrievers. And even though they did not complete the rigorous training program, they are all exceptionally well-behaved, already housebroken and intelligent. There is usually a long waiting list for these dogs, sometimes up to two years. If you don't mind the delay, you can call one of the many guide dog centers around the country and ask to be included on their waiting list. Since the cost of training a guide dog and master team is nearly $20,000, most centers request a donation to help offset these enormous costs.

PUPPY RAISERS

You can also obtain a FREE guide dog puppy from these schools to raise for 18 months. Since the guide dogs have to be well socialized before being trained for handicap work once they become an adult, the pups cannot be raised in a kennel environment. For this reason, guide dog centers commonly seek volunteers (usually called "puppy raisers") to take in the puppies, provide them with love, care, basic discipline and lots of socialization. In fact, puppy raisers are encouraged to take their puppy with them wherever they go, including the market, in office buildings, elevators and other public places.

Not everyone qualifies to be a puppy raiser, however. In most cases, the dog school first screens potential volunteers dur-

ing an interview. If you qualify, you are taught some basic obedience training techniques. You must then sign a contract that clearly states that the guide center owns the dog and can take the puppy away if they feel it is being raised improperly.

On the plus side, you get to raise a purebred dog and, in many cases, receive a discount on expenses, especially medical needs. (Each guide dog school varies somewhat on what expenses they pay.) Perhaps the greatest benefit, though, is that if your dog doesn't pass the rigorous training program, you get first right of refusal on adopting the dog yourself. Of course, if your dog does qualify for handicap work, you must say good-bye. Many people find this volunteer work very rewarding, especially when they formally give the dog to its new handicapped owner upon the dog's graduation.

The following is a list of guide dog centers that have both adoption programs: adult dog adoptions where the dog has been rejected from the program, and the puppy raising adoption program. Feel free to contact them for more information. They will gladly send you material about their program.

Canine Companions for Independence
P.O. Box 446
Santa Rosa, CA 95402
(707)579-1985

International Guiding Eyes, Inc.
13445 Glenoaks Blvd.
Sylmar, CA 91342
(818)362-5834

Guide Dogs For The Blind
P.O. Box 1299
San Rafael, CA 94915
(415)499-4000

Guide Dogs Of The Desert, Inc.
P.O. Box 1692
Palm Springs, CA 92262
(619)329-6257

Guide Dogs Of The Southeast
4210 77th Street E.
Palmetto, FL 34221
(813)729-5665

Leader Dogs For The Blind
1039 S. Rochester Road
Rochester, MI 48307
(313)651-9011

The Seeing Eye, Inc.
P.O. Box 375
Morristown, NJ 07963
(201)539-4425

Guiding Eyes For The Blind, Inc.
611 Granite Springs Road
Yorktown Heights, NY 10598
(914)878-3330

Pilot Dogs, Inc.
625 W. Town Street
Columbus, OH 43215
(614)221-6367

Paws With A Cause
Home of Ears For the Deaf, Inc.
1235 100th Street SE
Byron Center, MI
(616)698-0688

Canadian Guide Dogs For The Blind
P.O. Box 280
Manotick, Ontario, Canada
KOA 2NO
(613)692-7777

If you are interested in learning about hearing dogs, contact the Delta Society/American Humane Association Hearing Dog Resource Center at P.O. Box 1080, Renton, WA 98057-1080, (800)869-6898. Their service increases awareness and promotes access rights for hearing dogs used by the deaf and hard of hearing. They will send you a FREE copy of their pamphlet, *Hearing Dog Fact Sheet,* which explains what hearing dogs do, the cost involved and how to obtain one. They will also send you a FREE copy of their *Hearing Dog Training Center Directory* which lists hearing dog placement centers across the country.

One example of a hearing dog training center is Dogs for the Deaf, Inc. Their service enables hearing-impaired people to use specially trained dogs as their "ears" to the world, thereby giving them independence, freedom and constant companionship. Dogs are chosen from local animal shelters where they would otherwise be put to sleep. Following four months of training during which time they are taught to alert their owners to such everyday sounds as an alarm clock, a smoke alarm, a doorbell, specialized phones and even a baby's cry, the dogs are matched to their owners.

While the program's cost is $3,500 per dog, the service is provided FREE of charge to qualified applicants. For more information contact: Dogs for the Deaf, Inc., 10175 Wheeler Rd., Central Point, OR 97502, (503)826-9220.

PETS HELPING PEOPLE

Just as there are groups that place older or retired pets, there are also programs, funded through government grants or private donations, that provide companion pets for seniors. One example is Pets are Worth Saving of Hicksville, New York (a program through Pioneers for Animal Welfare Society). Representatives from these programs visit senior centers, retirement homes and retirement communities (accompanied by homeless pets) to help spread the word about their adoption services. Some programs even provide free veterinary services, cover the cost of neutering and supply transportation and food for those who can't afford the costs of owning a pet.

Pet Partners is a national registry of pets and volunteers who visit lonely, ill and disabled people. Pet Partners is offered by the Delta Society, an international non-profit organization that promotes beneficial relationships between animals and people and funds studies on how animals affect the mental and physical well-being of people. The project is sponsored by CIBA-

GEIGY Animal Health with support from the American Kennel Club and private donations. Pet partners include dogs, cats, birds and other pets. They accompany owners on visits to nursing homes, hospitals, schools, prisons, treatment centers and other facilities. For more information about the Pet Partners Program contact the Delta Society, P.O. Box 1080, Renton, WA 98057-1080, (206)226-7357.

PAWS/LA is a tax-exempt non-profit organization serving the Los Angeles area (there is also a program in San Francisco) that helps people with AIDS/ARC related disabilities keep their pets. This is one of the most compassionate, supportive services we have found. PAWS provides domestic pet care including walking, grooming, feeding and transportation to veterinary appointments. Their devoted volunteers find foster homes for pets when people with AIDS/ARC are hospitalized or unable to care for their pets. In addition, they provide pet food, supplies and assistance with acute care in emergency situations. When the need arises, they will also find permanent homes for pets, arranged in consultation with the owner who is given the opportunity to become acquainted with their pet's prospective new family. For information on PAWS/LA call (213)650-PAWS or in San Francisco (415)824-4040.

Similarly, Pet Owners with AIDS/ARC Resource Service Inc. (POWARS) operates in New York to help people with AIDS care for their pets. Their services include dog walking, vet care, counseling, grooming and in-home foster care. For information contact: POWARS, Inc., P.O. Box 1116, Madison Square Station, New York, NY 10159, (212)744-0842.

The Holistic Animal Consulting Centre, 29 Lyman Ave., Staten Island, NY 10303, provides information on companion animals for people diagnosed with AIDS. As pointed out by the executive director of the Centre, Barbara Meyers, for some people with AIDS, animal companions represent the only relationships that remain unaltered by the diagnosis.

ADOPTING A DIFFERENT KIND OF PET

In addition to dogs and cats, there are also horses, burros, rabbits, farm animals and even monkeys available for FREE adoption. When our daughter started horseback riding, we were able to obtain free, already-trained horses from a summer camp in exchange for feeding and giving them a home for the nine months of the year when they weren't being used by the camp. Later, she was given another good trail horse for free from a local resident who didn't have the time to ride anymore and wanted someone to exercise her horse and provide it with a good home. By keeping a lookout in the local papers, or even placing your own ad and asking neighborhood horse owners "to put the word out," there is a good chance that similar opportunities will present themselves.

The Bureau of Land Management (BLM) division of the federal government sponsors an "Adopt-A-Horse or Burro Program." The BLM is the agency responsible for managing the nation's herds of wild horses and burros. When the herds become too large for the range to support, some of the animals are rounded up and offered for adoption. More than 100,000 of them have been taken in by people. If you are interested in providing a home for a wild horse or burro write: Adopt-A-Horse, Bureau of Land Management, Dept. E, Room 5600 MIB, Washington, DC 20240, or call (202)343-5717. Most burros are easily tamed and quickly adapt to ranch or rural backyard living. Trained mustangs make excellent companions and trail horses.

The House Rabbit Society offers adoption of house rabbits. This is a national non-profit organization that arranges adoptions and distributes information on the care, feeding and health of rabbits. It also provides needy rabbits with food, housing, veterinary care and, eventually finds them permanent homes. House Rabbit Society rabbits are spayed or neutered, litterbox trained and socialized. The main office of the HRS is in Alameda, California, (415)521-4631. Branch offices are located in Los Angeles, (213)447-0593; Placerville, CA (619)644-2008; Redmond, WA (206)868-4839; Chicago, IL (312)643-0646; Bloomington, IN (812)333-3025; and Malabar, FL (305)724-6876.

Are you interested in adopting a farm animal? There are also rescue groups that place sheep, goats, hens and so on with good homes. Two examples are: Barnyard Rescue, (805)492-2127; and Farm Sanctuary, P.O. Box 37, Rockland, DE 19732, (302)654-9026. Barbara Bouyet, who operates Barnyard Rescue, places ducks, geese, pigs, cows, goats, etc. in ethical vegetarian homes. Barbara becomes so attached to her rescued friends that she maintains visitation rights with their adoptive families. Farm Sanctuary operates referral and placement services for abused and abandoned farm animals and participates in the Adopt-A-Farm-Animal program. The Fund for Animals (200 W. 57th Street, New York, NY 10019, (212)246-2096), in addition to using direct activism, legal action, public education and lobbying to protect wildlife and fight cruelty to animals, operates an Animal Trust Sanctuary in Ramona, CA, a shelter for dogs, cats and small feral animals. They also own and operate the Black Beauty Farm in Texas for homeless and abused horses.

If your tastes run towards the more exotic, contact the Simian Society of America, 3625 Watson Road, St. Louis, MO 63109, (314)647-6218. They are an adoption and relocation service for unwanted monkeys. Helping Hands, 1505 Commonwealth Ave., Boston, MA 02135, provides trained monkeys to disabled persons. They need foster homes to raise monkeys from six to eight weeks to three to four years of age. Foster families are reimbursed for medical care and are supplied with free food for the monkey.

HOME VIDEO SHOPPING FOR PETS

The recent craze in home video shopping has even branched into home pet shopping. One such show airs on cable television in Long Beach, CA. Twice a week host Fred Bergendorff of *The Pet Place* surrounds himself with a menagerie of barking, yowling, panting, scratching, sniffing pets looking for good homes and human companionship. The pets are from local animal shelters who are desperate to place the hoards of pets they rescue. Since *The Pet Place* began airing, responses at the shelters have increased more than 50 percent.

Kathy Macklem, Executive Director of the Cat Care Society, a Colorado no-kill shelter, tries to find good homes for cats through *Pet Line,* a local Denver television show which she tapes from her adoption facility, a suburban house with special outdoor enclosures. The *Pet Line* has been responsible for placing cats as old as 15 years in good homes. Call your local cable television company to see if any similar programs are broadcast in your area.

A FINAL WORD

Something you should know: pets from shelters and even those from pet shops have often received little, if any, recent health care and should have a thorough examination by a veterinarian within three days of purchase or adoption. Pets acquired through breeders run less risk of health problems since the breeders own both parents and can usually trace the animal's hereditary line through several generations. If your new pet is found to be unhealthy, the law requires the seller to refund or exchange it for another. However, make sure to get a bill of sale with your animal so that the seller can't claim your payment as an *adoption fee* and get around the law.

CHAPTER 3

To his dog, every man is Napoleon;
hence the constant popularity
of dogs.

--Aldous Huxley

FREE FOOD, TREATS & TOYS FOR YOUR PET

PLUS DISCOUNTS AND SAVINGS FOR FIDO AND FLUFFY

 The pet food and supply business is one of the largest, most competitive industries in this country. As we mentioned, pet-related spending will pass the $12 billion mark in the 1990s! By the year 2000, we will be spending nearly $8 billion of that for food for our pets. Currently there are 54.6 million household cats in the U.S., 52.4 million dogs and 12.9 million caged birds according to the Pet Food Manufacturers association. More than 53.4 percent of all U.S. households own some kind of pet.

EASY $$--COUPON YOUR WAY TO SAVINGS

How can we save money on the food, treats and toys we lavish on our beloved companions? The easiest way to save is as simple as reading your Sunday newspaper.

If you've ever glanced at the brightly colored coupon section of your Sunday newspaper, you know that coupons must be a big business. Why else would manufacturers spend millions of dollars advertising 10¢, 25¢, 50¢, $1.50 and more off their products? Because they want you to try their products and then become loyal, repeat customers.

Major supermarket brand pet food manufacturers advertise heavily in newspaper coupon sections. Lucky for us, theirs are among the most high-value coupons available. When you consider that many supermarkets double manufacturers coupons, you're talking about significant savings on your next purchase of dog or cat food. If you are not a brand-loyal shopper, you can use cents-off coupons nearly every time you shop. Many pets will gobble up any brand of food you give them and ask for more. They seem to thrive on whatever you put in front of them.

Some pets, however, require special diets. Some like variety in their meals or a combination of canned and dry food. Most manufacturers today make several varieties of pet foods formulated for a pet's health and age. Coupons are almost always good for any size or formula of a manufacturers product, so you can give your pet a specifically formulated diet and save money at the same time. Premium pet food manufacturers such as Iams, Science Diet and Nature's Recipe also offer savings on their products. You can find their coupons in the pages of pet magazines, newsletters and in pet stores that carry their brands. If you are interested in nutritional formulas or want more detailed information about a brand of food, write directly to the manufacturer and they will gladly send you lots of information about their products. In addition, nearly all companies will also include valuable discount coupons (without an expiration date) for use with your next purchase. These coupons are often worth several dollars off the retail price.

The following are examples of recently offered "cents-off" discounts for pet food products (remember, the value of these coupons are doubled at most supermarkets):

🐈 40¢ off one 3 1/2 lb. bag of Kitten Chow

🐈 30¢ off any size Kitten Chow

🐈 60¢ off on 12 cans of Fancy Feast gourmet canned cat food, any variety

🐕 35¢ off one package of Milk-Bone dog biscuits or T.C. biscuits

🐕 35¢ off one package of Milk-Bone T.C. rawhide strips

🐦 50¢ off Lafeber's Nutri-Berries bird food

🐕 40¢ off any size Sunshine dog or cat food

🐕 30¢ off any size package of Frosty Paws (a frozen treat made especially for dogs)

🐈 55¢ off any bag or two boxes of Friskies dry cat food

🐈 55¢ off on any size Friskies Kitten Formula dry kitten food

🐕 50¢ off on two bags of Lip Smackers (people cookies for dogs)

🐕 $4 off a 7 lb. or larger size bag of any Nutrix brand pet food blend

🐕 $2 off any size bag Pro Plan brand

🐈 $1 off on 3.5 lb. or larger Purina O.N.E. Optimum dog or cat formula

🐈 $2 off any 20 or 40 lb. size Pro Pac dog or cat foods

🐕 $2 off any Science Diet product with purchase of any size bag or six cans of any canine or feline Science Diet formula

🐈 50¢ off any 2 boxes of Pounce treats for cats

FREE FOOD ON YOUR TABLE AND IN YOUR PET'S BOWL

Nearly every week, along with the "cents-off" coupons, are dozens of offers for "FREE" products, often groceries, with a purchase of a brand pet food. The following are examples of recent "Free with Purchase" coupon offers:

🐕 FREE can of Pedigree Choice Cuts when you buy Pedigree Mealtime, 10 lb. bag or larger

🐕 FREE can of Grand Gourmet dog food (same size) when you buy three cans of Grand Gourmet, any size or variety

🐕 FREE Groceries (up to $1) when you buy any bag of Gaines Gravy Train

c. benjamin

🐕 FREE groceries (up to $1.50) with purchase of any size Chuck Wagon Lean dog food

🐕 FREE groceries (up to $3) with purchase of 18 lb. or larger bag of Purina Kibbles and Chunks dog food

🐕 FREE can, same size, when you buy four cans of Mighty Dog canned dog food, any size or variety

🐈 FREE groceries (up to $1.50) when you buy one 3.5 lb. bag or larger of any variety Purina O.N.E. pet food

🐕 FREE groceries (up to $1.50) with purchase of any size Purina Gravy dog food

🐕 FREE groceries (up to $1.50) with purchase of any size Purina Kibbles and Chunks dog food

🐈 FREE can with purchase of three cans of Friskies Kitten Formula canned kitten food, any variety

🐕 FREE can of Pedigree Food for Puppies when you buy any size bag of Pedigree Food for Puppies

🐕 FREE package of Snausages sausage style snacks for dogs with purchase of any bag of Kibbles 'n Bits dog food

🐕 FREE groceries (up to $2) with purchase of any size Nature's Course dog food

🐕 FREE groceries (up to $3) with purchase of 20 lb. or larger Nature's Course dog food

🐕 FREE groceries (up to $1) with purchase of 5 lb. or larger Purina Hi Pro dog food

🐕 FREE groceries (up to 75¢) with purchase of any size bag of Come 'N Get It dry dog food

🐕 FREE groceries (up to $1.50) with purchase of one 20 lb. bag or larger of Come 'N Get It dry dog food

🐕 FREE groceries (up to $1) with the purchase of any size Purina Puppy Chow puppy food

🐕 FREE groceries (up to $2) with the purchase of 20 lb. or larger Purina Puppy Chow puppy food

🐕 FREE groceries (up to $1.50) with purchase of any 20 or 25 lb. bag of Gaines Cycle Adult dog food

🐕 FREE groceries (up to $1) with purchase of any 5 or 10 lb. bag of Gaines Cycle Adult dog food

🐈 FREE groceries (up to 55¢) when you buy two boxes or one bag, any size, of Alpo Gourmet dinner or seafood flavor cat food.

🐈 FREE groceries (up to 75¢) when you buy two boxes or one bag of new Alpo seafood flavor cat food

🐕 FREE groceries (up to $1) with purchase of one 4,5,9,20 or 40 lb. bag of Purina Fit & Trim dog food

🐎 FREE 5 lbs. with every 50 lb. purchase of Omolene 100,200 or 300 formula for horses

🐕 FREE trial size Purina O.N.E. brand pet food or 79¢ off any variety of O.N.E.

🐈 FREE can of cat food with the purchase of five cans (any size) of Alpo Cat Food.

The following offers had a place on the coupon to write your name and address for additional money savings coupons and products by mail:

🐈 FREE can of 9 Lives Cat Food when you buy any ten cans

🐕 FREE can of Reward Dog Food when you buy two 3 oz. or one 6 oz. Jerky Treats dog snacks

🐐 FREE can Reward dog food when you buy Meaty Bone brand dog biscuits

🐐 FREE can 14 oz. Skippy Premium Dog Food when you buy any four cans of 14 oz. Skippy dog food

🐈 FREE can of Amore Gourmet cat food when you buy any two cans of Amore

🐈 Two FREE cans of 9 Lives cat food when you buy 9 Lives Crunch Meals, any size bag

🐈 FREE Friskies Calendar with Proofs of Purchase from qualifying cat food products

🐕 FREE Mighty Dog Calendar with Proofs of Purchase from qualifying dog food can labels

✂ MORE DISCOUNTS ON STUFF FOR YOUR PET . . .

In addition to savings on pet food and groceries, there are discounts on a variety of pet-related supplies. Some recent offers include:

🐕 $1 mail-in refund offer with proof of purchase from Shield flea and tick control for dogs and cats

🐈 Buy one, get one FREE, Ever Clean ES formula liquid waste remover for litter boxes

🐕 $1 off any 48-pack Dispoz-A-Scoop disposable pooper scoopers

🐈 40¢ off on a 7 or 16 lb. jug of Scoop Away advanced cat litter

🐈 50¢ off on any size Fresh Step cat litter

🐈 50¢ off any box of Arm & Hammer Carpet deodorizer

🐈 25¢ off purchase of 5.5 lb. Super Sand cat litter

🐈 40¢ off on Purina Cat Chow self-feeder

🐈 25¢ off any Cardinal product (shampoo products for dogs)

🐈 Buy two jugs of Super Sand, miracle cat litter at regular price and get one free

🐈 30¢ off purchase of any size Cat's Pride original cat litter

Also, look for mail-in refund and rebate offers (often advertised next to "cents-off" coupons) for pet food and supplies. These are usually good for cash refunds of $1 to $4 or more with proof of purchase.

ABSOLUTELY FREE--SAMPLE GOODIES, TREATS & MORE

These are the best. Free samples and trial size offers of every imaginable pet food, treat and goodie. Over the past year we have collected a small mountain of freebies that would fill most kitchen pantries. Where do they come from? Pet stores, pet shows, veterinary clinics, feed stores, spay and neuter clinics sponsored by pet food manufacturers, breeders and by contacting manufacturers directly. In most cases, all you have to do is walk in and ask for samples. They're there for the taking.

Many food samples are high-quality, scientifically formulated products recommended by veterinarians and breeders. With most animal professionals recommending that pets be fed a "life stage" diet, collecting samples and trying them is a great way to find out which kind agrees with your pet. Try different foods and food combinations. When you have found a healthy, balanced diet your pet likes, stick with it.

The following pet food manufacturers will send you FREE samples of cat and dog food. Be sure to let them know how old your pet is. Those that don't send out samples will tell you where you can get them nearby.

Hills Science Diet: (800)633-6357
NutroMax: (800)367-2391; (800)833-5330
Iams & Eukanuba: (800)525-4267; (800)255-4738, ext. 405
Purina: (800)PRO-PLAN; (800)323-4ONE
Nature's Recipe: (800)843-4008
Martin TechniCal: (800)265-3370

☆ Purina will send you a 10 oz. FREE SAMPLE of Fit & Trim adult dog food. Write them at: Purina Fit & Trim FREE Sample Offer, P.O. Box 15344, Mascoutah, IL 62224. They will also send you a FREE 7.5 oz. sample of Purina O.N.E. dog formula. Call them at (800)323-4ONE, ext. 200.

☆ Gaines foods will send you a sample of beef or cheese flavored Tastee-Chunk snack food for dogs. Write to: Gaines Foods, Inc., Box 4805, Kankakee, IL 60902.

☆ The Lafeber Company wants you to try a sample of their quality bird food. Call them at (800)332-3542.

Would you like to serve your dog a FREE hot meal? Our local pet store was offering a FREE lamb & rice loaf meal from Breeder's Choice. Check with your local pet store to see if they carry Breeder's Choice dog food and are promoting the same offer.

Manufacturers will often tie in with a local supplier to get customers to try their brand. In this case they will supply the pet store with free products and the store passes the free offer on to the public, either through a mailer or advertisement. One recent offer consisted of a free 5 lb. bag of dog food or a free 3 lb. bag of cat food. No other purchase was necessary.

☆ Along with a recent $3 off rebate offer, Science Diet gave special coupon-bearing customers a free trial-size bag of any Science Diet Formula for dogs or cats.

☆ J.E. Ronicker Laboratories will send you a free sample of Xtrabloom Wate, a powdered fat for cats that aids weight gain, improves coats and makes food more palatable. If you are concerned whether your cat is getting enough vitamins and minerals, they will include a sample of Kitty Bloom VM900+2, an advanced formula cat supplement. Call them at (800)833-4748.

☆ Natural Life Pet Products use no artificial preservatives, meat by-products, sugar or nitrates and nitrites. For a FREE sample of their formulated product (let them know if you have a dog or a cat), call them at (800)367-2391.

☆ Do you own or breed Lories (a type of bird)? John Vanderhoff, P.O. Box 575, Woodlake, CA 93286, will send you a free sample of Lories Delight Dry Diet in powder form, natural to Lories. He also breeds and has written a book on Lories and Lorikeets.

☆ Blair's Super Preen for all birds promotes growth, performance, beauty and breeding. Super Preen's manufacturer, RHB Laboratories, will send you a free sample to try with your bird. Call RHB at (800)421-8239.

In addition to pet food samples, you can also receive samples of other pet related products. For example:

☆ Arm & Hammer, the folks who have shown us the many uses of baking soda as a natural deodorizer, distribute generous samples of Pet Fresh, carpet & room deodorizing powder and air freshener to veterinary offices and clinics.

☆ The White Horse Trading Co. is the maker of high quality rubber mats for horses. Call them at (800)STALMAT for a sample of their shock block protector stall mat.

☆ Lactaid is a lactose reduced lowfat milk formula for cats (and humans) who can't digest milk. The Lactaid lactase enzyme makes milk's lactose digestible. For a FREE sample call (800)LAC-TAID.

☆ Dri-Dek interlocking floor tiles keeps animals drier, cleaner and more comfortable in their cages, runs and pens. The cushioned tiles are also treated with antibacterial agents that help fight infection. For a FREE sample kit call (800)348-2398.

☆ A FREE single-wash sample of the world's richest super concentrated luxury conditioning shampoo for dogs is available from Mr. Christal's, 270 No. Canon Drive, #1297, Beverly Hills, CA 90210. Enclose $1 for postage and handling to receive your sample of Mr. Christal's Australian Luxury shampoo for dogs.

By far, the greatest amount of FREE samples are available at pet shows, pet and feed stores and veterinary clinics. Most places will allow you to take generous helpings of the samples on display. After all, if your pet likes the FREEBIES, they're hoping you'll come back and buy more of their product. The following are some of the FREE samples we picked up during a couple of days of "shopping":

☆ FROM SCIENCE DIET
Free Nutrition Kits that teach owners about preventive health care for their pets. Kits include a generous food sample, Health Record card, facts on your pet at his stage of life and a detailed guide to preventive health care. Science Diet makes kits for active adult dogs, puppies, kittens, older dogs, adult dogs, adult cats and overweight adult cats.

☆ FROM PURINA
Free trial size dog food samples of Purina Pro Plan Lite Formula, Adult Formula, Performance Formula, Growth Formula and trial size samples of Adult Formula cat food.

☆ FROM WYSONG DISTRIBUTING
Free samples of Junior Growth for dogs, Feline Vitality for cats and Adult Maintenance for dogs.

☆ FROM IAMS
Free 6-oz. sample cartons of Chunks for dogs, Less Active for dogs, Puppy Food, Mini Chunks for dogs, Cat Food and Less Active for cats.

☆ FROM EUKANUBA
Free 6 oz. samples of Eukanuba for Puppies, Eukanuba for dogs, Adult Eukanuba Maintenance for dogs and Growth Eukanuba for puppies.

☆ FROM NUTRO
FREE samples of Max Special for senior, less active and overweight dogs; Max Cat lite for less active, neutered and spayed cats; Max kibble dog food for adult dogs; Natural Choice lamb and rice formula dog food; Max Puppy and Max Cat.

☆ FROM NATURE'S RECIPE
Free 4 and 6 oz. samples of Optimum Feline Diet Lite, Non-meat kibble dog food, Lamb and Rice kibble dog food, Senior/Pension dog food and Optimum Feline Diet.

☆ FROM BREEDER'S CHOICE
Free samples of Complete wheat base dog food (trial size), Puppy Formula (trial size) and AVO-DERM dog food (for healthy skin and coats).

☆ FROM MARTIN TECHNI-CAL
Free samples of Techni-Cal cat food (120 gms), Techni-Cal senior dog food (200 gms), Techni-Cal growth dog food (200 grams) and Techni-Cal mini maintenance dog food (200 grams.).

In addition we also picked up these freebies:

- Starter dose of Pet-Tabs/F.A. for Dogs and Cats (vitamin granules and tablets) from Beecham Laboratories

- Complimentary first bath Mycodex Pet Shampoo for Cats and Dogs

- Sample Dispoz-A-Scoop pooper scooper from Petpro Products

- Sample Flea Stop shampoo (1 fl. oz.) from Terminix

- A sample of "Cat Love," the happy, healthy cat treat from Hagen

- Trial size sample (6 oz.) of dog food chunks from Sunshine

- A generous 1/2 lb. sample of the Abady formula dog food for maintenance and stress

- Waffle-shaped beef basted dog biscuits (2.2 oz.) from Wagtime

- Trial size sample of Lafeber's Nutri-Berries cockatiel food

- From Hikari, makers of fancy goldfish (koi) products: samples of wheat germ gold fish & koi food, cichlid Excel fish food wheat germ & spirulina formula, chiclid staple complete balanced nutrition fish food and Hikari excell color enhancing food for koi

🐢 A 2 oz. sample of Aquatic Turtle Food and 2.5 oz. sample of Hermit Crab Food from Zoo Menu

🐠 Samples of Amo Chlor, fresh water and marine water conditioner and Shieldex, fresh and marine water conditioner

🐠 50 oz. gm. sample of Swimny Premium Blend koi food from Nippon Pet Food Co.

MORE SAVINGS ON TREATS AND TOYS

In the past, many manufacturers of pet toys and treats offered free samples to individuals for little more than the cost of postage and handling. Unfortunately, the days of free samples from the "big guys" seem to be over. Because of tighter economics, most of them now distribute only to retail stores and catalogs. However, through our research we have discovered several smaller manufacturers who will still honor pet lovers with free (or nominally priced) toys that you can send away for.

☆ Wow-Bow Distributors has created a full line of health treats for pets, including health foods, books, biscuits and other items. Hand cut and freshly baked, all their biscuits contain only the finest natural ingredients. Indicate whether you own a cat, dog or horse and they will send you a free sample of these nutritious, delicious biscuits. Write to: Wow-Bow Distributors, Ltd., 309 Burr Road, East Northport, NY 11731.

☆ The Waggle Button is a homemade button on a string of yarn guaranteed to keep your cat entertained for hours. This unique toy is available for just 75¢ plus $1.25 shipping and handling. Write: Gracie Horyna, 1624 2nd, Great Bend, KS 67530.

☆ Supplement your pet's meals with nutritious vitamin, mineral and yeast snacks that they will love. If you are a dog owner, you can use these treats to reward your dog for good behavior. For a free sample of dog or cat Snap Treats, enclose $1 for shipping and handling to: Losvet, P.O. Box 2473, Beverly Hills, CA 90213.

☆ Send for a packet of catnip seeds so you can grow your own catnip. You can make your own cat toys and save lots of dollars by stuffing the catnip inside plastic balls, old socks, etc. Send $1.50 plus 30¢ shipping charges (CA residents add 8.25% tax) to Taylor's Herb Garden, 1535 Lane Oak Road, Vista, CA 92804.

☆ Taylor's also wants to help you keep flies and parasites, such as fleas, away from you pet with their Pennyroyal herb seeds. The price is the same as the catnip seeds. For both seed packets send $3.00 plus 30¢ shipping charges (CA residents add 8.25% tax) to Taylor's Herb Garden at the above address.

☆ Famous Fido's produces all natural dog and catnip cookies that contain no preservatives, artificial flavoring and no animal fats or by-products. For a sample, enclose $1.50 to: Famous Fido's, Inc. 1527 West Devon, Chicago, IL 60660. They ship worldwide.

CHAPTER 4

It's true, you can never eat a pet
you name. And anyway, it would
be like a ventriloquist
eating his dummy.

--Alexander Theroux

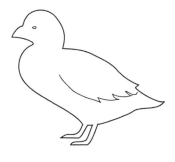

FREE AND LOW-COST HEALTH CARE SERVICES FOR YOUR PET

 Most pets probably feel the same way we do about going to the doctor. Neither of us like it and we try to avoid it whenever possible. I know that as soon as I put one foot in the veterinarian's office, my dogs put on the skids and run the other way.

In addition to our mutual feelings of "What Am I Doing Here?" and "I Should Be Outside Playing," few of us love paying those rising medical costs, for either ourselves or our pets. Of course, there's medical insurance for us (although still a costly expense) and, as we discuss in Chapter 5, there's also medical insurance for our pets (a more reasonably priced alternative).

There are also several other money-saving alternatives when it comes to health care for our pets, especially for the more common treatments and preventative medical care that insures our pets stay happy and healthy. These include spay and neuter services, health exams and evaluations and vaccination clinics.

DO THE RIGHT THING: CONTROL PET OVERPUPULATION

Pet overpopulation is an enormous problem that can only be solved and brought under control by spaying and neutering your pets. Every five minutes another 250 dogs and cats are born (that translates to almost 3,000 dogs and cats born every hour, compared to 400 human births an hour). In the U.S. alone, more than 15 million animals are brought into municipal and private animal shelters each year. Many of these animals are strays or abandoned, brought in by animal control officers or concerned citizens. Many others are brought in by their owners who, for a variety of reasons, are unable to keep them. It is impossible for these overcrowded, overburdened shelters to find homes for all of them. As a result, nearly 70 percent, almost 11 million dogs and cats, puppies and kittens, must be destroyed because no one wants them. In addition, over $500 million in taxpayer money is spent to fund this unfortunate cycle.

The best way to reduce the number of pets that are being destroyed is to reduce the number of puppies and kittens being born. There are also other benefits to spaying and neutering your pets including:

🐱 Your pet will be a more content, lovable family member.

🐶 Your pet will be healthier, saving you money at the vet's and, on average, will live longer.

🐱 Your pet will stay closer to home, avoiding injury due to traffic accidents or fights with other animals.

🐶 Your pet will not be frustrated by biological drives to reproduce.

🐱 Your pet will be better behaved.

🐶 Your pet's license will cost at least 50 percent less.

😺 You won't have to find homes for your pet's offspring.

In addition to the long-term savings in veterinary bills (both for your pet and its future offspring), spay/neutering costs are available at very affordable rates. Due to the widespread support and encouragement from humane educators, S.P.C.A.s and humane societies, veterinarians, animal shelter workers, ethical dog and cat breeders and informed pet owners, low-cost surgeries have become available nearly everywhere.

FREE clinics for qualified senior citizens and low income individuals are sponsored by most city or county Animal Regulation and Animal Care and Control departments. Public shelters and pounds also give rebates and refunds to people who adopt animals and then come back with their adoption receipts and sterility certificates proving that they've had their pet altered.

Humane Societies, S.P.C.A.'s and hundreds of other non-profit groups nationwide offer periodic low cost clinics to pet owners. (In Los Angeles, the S.P.C.A. offers a FREE "Litter Abatement Program.") Some pet stores and veterinary hospitals also team up to offer low cost spay/neutering services.

Friends of Animals is a national non-profit group that enlists the services of licensed veterinarians across the country for their Breeding Control Program. They issue Breeding Control Certificates for reduced cost sterilizations valid at any participating veterinary clinic. For certificate order forms and a list of veterinarians call (800)631-2212. Many local non-profit groups offer certificate/coupon/rebate programs with participating vets who discount their regular spay/neuter services 50 percent or more.

KEEPING FIDO AND FLUFFY HEALTHY--FOR FREE

Many times pets from shelters have received little, if any, recent health care. Even if you buy your pet from a pet store or reputable breeder, there may be no guarantee that it is healthy and free from disease or internal problems. Most vets recommend having your new pet examined thoroughly within two to three days of purchase or adoption, and some suggest bringing your new pet in within 24 hours of adoption.

Nearly every veterinary clinic we surveyed offered a FREE "new pet" exam with proof of adoption from a licensed shelter, humane society or adoption agency. Check your local veterinary clinic about their free health exam policy. The regular charge for a complete exam and evaluation generally costs between $25 to $35.

In support of pet adoption through recognized agencies and rescue groups, The Veterinary Centers of America, Inc., a group of 12 animal hospitals located in Southern California, Arizona and Colorado, offer FREE exams for any pet adopted through *Muttmatchers* magazine. For information on locations of member animal hospitals call (213)829-7533.

LOW-COST VACCINATION CLINICS

Low-cost vaccination clinics are one of the easiest, most convenient money-saving opportunities you can find. Keeping your pets' vaccines and annual boosters current is essential to protect them from dangerous pet diseases. As a pet owner, you know that there are no less than five routine vaccines needed by dogs and four for cats including rabies, 6-in-1 (dogs) 4-in-1 (cats), parvo, corona virus, bordetella, feline leukemia, chlamydia, distemper and tests and treatments for heartworms, tapeworms and roundworms. Individually, these vaccines and tests can cost up to $25 each.

Luckily, there are a number of ways to save on these costly but necessary health measures. Recognizing the fact that many people cannot afford the regular cost of vaccinations (and, therefore thousands of pets might run the risks of carrying and spreading potentially deadly diseases), some private veterinarians offer special low-cost vaccine clinics on a weekly or monthly basis. These are usually held on weekends or evenings when they won't interfere with regular office hours.

Your city or county Department of Animal Regulation and Control or local Humane Society may offer free or low cost clinics at local parks, community centers or pet stores.

Pet Vaccine Services, Inc. is a specialized company that offers low-cost vaccinations for dogs and cats through their mobile clinics. Over 400 clinics a month are held in pet stores and other locations, such as department and grocery store parking lots in Arizona, Southern California, Texas, Oregon, Nevada and Washington. Most clinics are held Saturdays and Sundays and some evenings. Vaccinations are performed by state-licensed veterinarians and written certification is provided to each pet owner. To find a clinic in your area call

(800)3-DOG-CAT or check for an announcement in your news-paper.

By taking advantage of these special services, you can save up to 60 percent off the regular price for a series of pet vac-cines. In order to make the public aware of these clinics, pet stores, hospitals and public agencies advertise their dates and times in local newspapers.

You can also call your vet or nearby pet supply store for the date of the next scheduled low-cost clinic.

CHAPTER 5

No animal should ever jump on
the dining-room furniture unless
absolutely certain that he can
hold his own in conversation.

--Fran Lebowitz

SAVINGS ON OTHER PET SERVICES

The responsibility for a pet doesn't stop with providing food, shelter, health care, hugs and treats now and then. For both you and your pet's benefit, well-being and comfort there are other services you may need from time to time. In the following chapter we will look at these services, including pet-sitting and boarding, grooming and flea control, pet loss support groups, animal training and pet insurance, plus some specialized services. Discounts and money-saving opportunities are available if you are willing to spend time researching your options. It will be worth your while to learn as much as possible about the services offered in your area. Here are some examples and ideas to get you started.

INSURANCE FOR YOUR PET?
SAVING MONEY IN THE LONG RUN

Did you know?

☞ Veterinary medical costs for animals climbed 183 percent from 1981 to 1986 while expenditures for humans increased approximately 59 percent.

☞ There are over 6,400 medical diseases and problems that occur in pets.

☞ Nearly 40 percent of all visits to the veterinarian by dogs and cats are due to sudden illness or emergencies.

☞ The current cost for medical procedures as a result of an automobile accident to your pet could cost $1000, cancer diagnosis and treatment over $2500 and intestinal tract problems over $1000.

☞ The chances of your pet suffering a serious illness or accident during its lifetime are 50/50.

Many pet owners are still unaware of the existence of pet insurance which is rapidly gaining acceptance as veterinary fees rise. Today's sophisticated medical diagnoses and procedures have made it possible to save animals where euthanasia would have been the only option a few years ago. In a nutshell, having pet insurance in the case of an accident or serious illness can make the economic difference between saving your pet's life or putting him to sleep.

Most people don't realize how much veterinary care can cost until it's too late and they are forced to make immediate medical and economic decisions. Routine vaccinations and exams (if paid for through low-cost and discount programs) can lead us to believe that animal medical care is affordable on a once or twice-a-year basis. And it usually is. However, when something unexpected happens to your pet, carrying pet insurance takes away the specter of unaffordability and lets you focus on what's best and necessary for your pet.

Like human medical insurance, pet insurance does not cover ordinary, routine medical care such as vaccinations, certain pre-existing conditions and illnesses, elective neutering, cosmetic surgery, grooming and normal checkups. Preventable diseases (those for which vaccines are available) are also not covered.

There are two major companies in the pet insurance field: Animal Health Insurance Agency Inc. (AHIA) and Veterinary Pet Insurance.

AHIA sells the Medipet Plan underwritten by Lloyd's of London and The Fireman's Fund in 49 states and throughout Canada. Premiums for dogs and cats are the same. Kittens must be at least three months old to be insured and all other pets are insured for illness and injury up to ten years old. After age ten a pet is insurable for injury only.

They offer two plans: Plan A, comprehensive illness and injury health coverage, for $99/year, per pet covers up to $1000 per injury or illness with a $50 deductible; Plan B, catastrophic illness and injury coverage, costs $42/year, per pet and pays up to $2500 per injury or illness after a $250 deductible. Once the deductible is satisfied, the company pays for 70 percent of all covered costs. The plan also pays for hospitalization up to $20 a day until the third day and 50 percent up to $10 a day thereafter. For more information about AHIA's plans, call (800)345-6778. (Another agency, Grossinger & Heller of Red Bank, NJ, also offers the Medipet Plan. Contact them at (201)741-2100 to compare their rates with AHIA.)

Veterinary Pet Insurance (VPI) was started in 1980 by a group of veterinarians who were frustrated by the number of pets being put to sleep for economic reasons. Their altruistic reasons for starting a pet insurance company have grown into a business which has since sold more than 250,000 pet insurance policies and has satisfied more than $4 million in claims. The company hopes to be licensed in all 50 states by the end of 1991 (they are presently licensed in 34 states). VPI offers three policies for pet protection covering everything from ear infections and abscesses to cancer and heart disease: 1) Major Medical Plan 20 requires a $20 deductible and insures puppies and kittens from two to 11 months for $44, from one to four years for $54 and from five to eight years for $69 (one year premiums); 2) Major Medical Plan 40 has a $40 deductible and costs

$29 for puppies and kittens for one year of coverage, $37 for pets aged one to four years and $47 for dogs and cats from five to eight years old; and 3) VPI Gold Plan, designed for pet owners who want the choice of higher medical insurance coverage, benefits and protection for their pets, pays up to $1000 per illness or accident and up to $7500 per policy year. There is a $40 deductible and premiums range from $79 up to $129 per year. VPI pays for 80 percent of the first $180 and 100 percent in excess of $180 per incident (after the deductible has been met) for all three plans.

Recently, VPI and Friskies PetCare Products teamed up to offer a special discount program for purchasers of Friskies PetCare Products. To enroll by phone or for more information about VPI's programs, call (800)USA-PETS.

The growing public awareness of how current state-of-the-art veterinary care can improve a pet's quality of life, the rising cost of pet health care and the evolution of the human/animal bond all contribute to the argument that pet insurance is a viable consideration. Having insurance may not only save you money, but it will also most likely help you in making an important decision if the need ever arises.

Before I leave the topic of insurance, I would like to mention that there are several agencies that provide horse insurance policies. Horses, in addition to being great family pets for pleasure riding, are also an investment, especially if you or your children develop an interest in showing. The value of prize winning horses can range from $3,000 to $300,000. The following are agencies that will cover your horse for mortality, major medical, surgery, theft and loss of use.

🐎 Paoli Insurance Agency, Inc., 16 Industrial Blvd., Suite 110B, P.O. Box 957, Paoli, PA 19301

🐎 Carl Weil Insurance, P.O. Box 525, Kiowa, CO 80117

🐎 Blue Bridle, P.O. Box 27, Pittstown, NJ 08867

🐎 Equisport/Ralph C. Wilson Agency, Inc., 201 W. Big Beaver Rd., Suite 1100, Troy, MI 48084

🐎 Newton Baker Insurance Services, Inc., P.O. Box 247, Lakeview, NC 28350

🐎 Ziplow Horse Insurance, 2209 Maryland Avenue, Baltimore, MD 21218

🐎 The Silverwood Agency, P.O. Box 2384, Grapevine, TX 76051

🐎 Kiger & Associates, Inc., One Tabor Center, 1200 17th Street, Suite 2330, Denver, CO 80202

The North American Horsemen's Association also offers insurance as one of their membership benefits. For information write: North American Horsemen's Association, Administrative Offices, Ark International Group, P.O. Box 223, Paynesville, MN 56362, (800)328-8894.

PET SITTING AND BOARDING: WHAT TO DO WITH YOUR PET WHEN YOU TRAVEL

Up until a few years ago, the only alternative to leaving your pets when you went out of town was either to board them in a kennel or entrust their care and feeding with a neighborhood kid or friend. If your pet was the sort that didn't respond well to a kennel environment (not to mention the possibility of exposure to illnesses from other animals), being placed in new surroundings or you didn't quite trust the neighbor's teenager with your precious companion, neither of these alternatives were satisfactory. Enter the pet-sitting industry.

Pet-sitting is a rapidly growing service industry that offers much the other two alternatives do not. Professional pet sitters come to your home and provide a number of services during an average 30 or 40 minute visit. These include: walking your dogs, feeding your pets, bringing in the mail, turning lights on and off, watering plants, forwarding mail and spending quality play time with your pets. Some pet sitters will also provide transportation services such as taking your pet to and from the vet, dropping a pet off at the vet or taking him to the groomer. Some will even sleep at your home, making sure your pet has company through the night and in the morning.

Fees for pet sitting services vary. Most day visits last approximately 40 minutes and cost between $10–$15 a visit. Depending on your pet's needs, you can have daily or twice daily visits. There are several ways you can find a reliable, reputable pet sitter that provides at-home pet care in your area. First, visit pet shops, groomers and veterinary clinics in your neighborhood and pick up pet-sitter brochures or ask them who they recommend. Also, check their bulletin boards for flyers and cards. Your local newspaper might have ads for pet/house sitting services. The Humane Society in your area may have a pet-sitters registry and referral service. There are also organizations that act as information and referral services for member pet-sitters. Some of these include:

- Pet Sitters Association of Southern California, P.O. Box 5432, Whittier, CA 90607-5432

- National Association of Pet Sitters, 632 Holly Ave., Winston-Salem, NC 27101, (919)723-PETS

- American Petsitting Club (referral service, fee), 61 S. Division St., New Rochelle, NY 10805, (800)765-7400

- Home Sitting Seniors, Inc. is a national distributorship with more than 20 service offices around the country. Responsible, retired mature adults provide home-sitting, pet-sitting and non-medical companion care for on-the-go owners. For more information, contact the national corporate office, (303)761-1878. Ask for Al Sutherland.

If it makes you more comfortable, choose a professional pet-sitter who is licensed as an Animal Care Consultant, bonded and insured. However, some of the most highly regarded pet care services rely entirely on word of mouth and satisfied client recommendations without regard to certification. Always compare services as well as fees when considering a pet sitter.

Forget everything you may have heard about strange acting Norman Bates-type people who run questionable animal kennels with worse than prison conditions. Animal kennels have come a long way from the days when you would leave to go on vacation and hoped your pet survived the trip. Animal boarding facilities run the gamut from normal to extraordinary services, depending on what you need for your pet and what you are willing to pay. Just as there are all classes of human accommodations from budget motels to fantasy-island luxury resorts, so do kennels range from very modest, but clean and safe, to the ultimate in "home-away-from-homes" for your pet. Rates vary according to amenities and services as they do for human accommodations. Consider the following services offered by various kennels:

- Three-room suites and condos with attached enclosed patios and/or sunning windows

- 24-hour, on-call veterinary supervision

- Indoor recreation room with television and human companions

- Special diets and medication or healthy, nutritious house diet

- Pet limousine pick-up and relocation service

- Daily playtime and treats

- Temperature controlled environment

- Hotline protection to police and fire stations

🐕 Clean, soft, non-allergic bedding changed daily

🐈 Spa packages, including: pet massage, puppy/kitten care, exercise program, special grooming, geriatric program

🐕 24-hour residential staff on duty

Does this sound better than your own vacation plans? Seriously, pet kennels (also referred to as Kitty Kastles, Holiday Hotels and Kennel Clubs) want your business and need your recommendations and referrals. However, as always, compare prices for what you need and carefully consider the "extras." Ask your friends for personal recommendations to help you in your search for a trustworthy boarding facility. Also, check with your veterinarian (he may offer boarding without all the frills) or a local pet store.

If you absolutely MUST travel with your pet, there are hotels and motels that accept animals (this is the norm in Europe, but less acceptable in the U.S.). The swank Ambassador East hotel in Chicago recently made available a VIPets service, with six rooms and two suites set aside as pet pads. At the Ambassador maids turn down the blankets on cushiony pet beds (and their owners' beds as well) and leave a milk bone for a guest dog or a toy for a cat. In addition, guest dogs receive a bag of treats and customized feeding bowl, while cats get a scratching post and litter box. Owners are also given pooper scoopers for neighborhood walks and 24-hour veterinarian and grooming services. The VIPets service costs $15 a night.

On the West Coast, the San Ysidro Ranch, an elegant, country resort in Santa Barbara, allows dogs to stay with their owners in any of their suites. They require a $100 refundable damage deposit and charge $35 to de-flea the room once you and your pet depart.

If your vacation plans include bringing Fido along, you might want to check through *Traveling with Towser,* a listing of pet-tolerant accommodations nationwide published by Quaker Oats. For a copy send $1.50 to Professional Services, P.O. Box 877, Young America, MN 55399. You can also send $5 to 9

Greenmeadow Dr. #FD, N. Billerica, MA 01862-1921 for a *Pets Allowed* directory of places to stay nationwide. Similiarly, the *Pet Travel Guide* is another nationwide hotel/motel directory of places that permit pets. Send $7.50 to JPS, P.O. Box 66006, W. Des Moines, IA 50265.

Petfinders, a lost-pet locator service, also acts as a modified travel agency. If you send them your itinerary, they will send you listings of hotels that welcome both pets and owners, as well as information about quarantines or other domestic/international restrictions, disease alerts and updates on dog and cat shows. Membership is $29.50 for the first year, $10 thereafter. To register, call Petfinders at (800)666-5678.

For additional information about boarding and kennels contact these national membership organizations:

☆ American Boarding Kennels Association
4575 Galley Road, Suite 400-A
Colorado Springs, CO 80915
(719)591-1113

☆ American Pet Boarding Association
P.O. Box 931
Wheeling, IL 60090
(708)634-9447

For a FREE directory on *Where to Buy, Board and Train a Dog* write to: Gaines Kennel Directory, Box 8177, Kankakee, IL 60902. This useful guide lists and describes the services of thousands of kennels across the U.S.

Among the information provided by the American Pet Boarding Association are the "Ten Commandments of Pet Boarding" which are excellent guides to follow when choosing a boarding facility. They are:

I.
Thou shalt not board in any facility that will not let you see where your pet will be kept.

II.

Thou shalt not board in any facility that boards or treats sick animals in the same general area as are kept boarded pets.

III.

Thou shall not board in any facility that is not clean and well maintained inside and outside.

IV.

Thou shalt not board in any facility that does not require proof of proper vaccinations.

V.

Thou shalt not board in any facility that employs immature or incompetent employees to clean and care for the animals.

VI.

Thou shalt not board your dog in a cage or pen unless you know it will receive three fifteen minute exercise periods daily, regardless of the weather.

VII.

Thou shalt not board your pet in a facility that lacks properly designed ventilation to maintain the ambient temperature between 65° F and 85° F for all warm blooded animals.

VIII.

Thou shalt not board your pet in a facility that will not contact your own veterinarian in event of a serious illness or injury.

IX.

Thou shalt not board your pet in a facility that does not feed the animals and clean and disinfect their accommodations as required and never less than once in every 24-hour period for warm blooded animals.

X.
Thou shalt not board your pet in a facility that permits the boarding of different owners' pets in the same space.

SENDING YOUR PET TO SCHOOL

All dogs, cats and many birds require training of some kind in order to live harmoniously with their human families. (Horses and other ranch and farm animals need extensive training as well, but we've limited our discussion to pets *in* the home.) The desire for a pleasurable, faithful, trustworthy companion and pet is the primary reason most people choose to have an animal in their home. Cute little kittens and puppies only stay "cute" for a short time. Sooner than you think, they've grown into full size animals who believe—since your home is their home—they can behave in any wild, unruly and destructive way they please. Dogs, especially, can be trained beginning as early as seven weeks of age, thus preventing most adult behavior and obedience problems.

Training cats and birds is usually related to specific problems, habits or behaviors that are unacceptable. Some are taught particular tricks or specialty stunts. In the case of birds, many owners hire professional trainers to teach them to talk. There are also many books and videos on the subjects of taming and training particular species to talk and do tricks. Check with pet shops that specialize in birds for recommendations of personal trainers. They can aid you in taming your pet as well as give you advice on breeding, choosing a bird, health, nutrition, housing and grooming.

Since the majority of pet training services is for dogs, we are going to focus on the methods and choices available. There are a wide variety of philosophies regarding dog training that can range in cost accordingly. Basically, you can train your pet in one of three ways:

🐾 **In-home training.** The trainer comes to your home for a series of sessions and trains you and your pet(s) in the familiar surroundings of your family and home.

🐾 **Away from home training with owner.** You and your pet go to a facility (training school, playground, community center or park) and receive your training together in a series of classes.

🐾 **Away from home training without owner.** You send your pet to be trained at a boarding "dog school" for a specific length of time.

Or, in addition, you can use:

🐾 **Telephone training.** A few highly trained animal behaviorists and psychotherapists will counsel pet owners about behavioral problems over the phone.

Training programs are also developed for dogs according to their age and whether they have specific problems that need to be eliminated. These are generally broken down into: Puppy training (from 7-16 weeks); Basic adult obedience training (16 weeks and up); and problem-solving training (i.e. jumping on people, chewing, aggression, running away or into the street, excessive barking, etc.). Obedience training can include both on-leash or more advanced off-leash training, in addition to teaching basic commands. There are also specialized training programs for theatrical and stunt work, protection, guide dogs and hunting dogs.

Often when a pet's environment changes drastically, as when moving to a new home, the arrival of a new baby or the departure of a principal companion, they need to be acclimated to these stressful changes. There's special training for these situations as well. In-home training programs are individualized, one to two hour sessions where the trainer comes to your home, often working with different members of your family to train your pet. The comfortable, familiar surroundings are conducive to training as the pet may be more relaxed and able to concentrate on his lessons. Also, specific problems that occur at home can be dealt with in the same surroundings in which they occur.

Most courses run from five to ten weeks and cost between $300–$1200 for a complete once-a-week program. Some trainers also offer individual sessions for problems that may not require a whole series. In these cases they charge a set hourly or per-session rate. Most trainers offer a FREE consultation to evaluate your pet. When choosing an "in-home" program, make sure the trainer guarantees his work and will retrain you and your dog free of charge at any time if backsliding occurs.

The most familiar (and least expensive) example of away-from-home training with an owner are puppy and dog training classes offered by city and county Parks and Recreation Departments. They are usually taught by private professional trainers who offer these low-cost classes to the public. The classes take place at school playgrounds, parks, community centers or other public places. Classes usually meet once a week in the evening, making it convenient for those who work during the day. One positive element of this type of training is that your dog becomes socialized and learns to behave around other animals in a class with ten or more other dogs. However, if your dog is easily distracted, having this many new friends around may keep you and him from concentrating on the lesson at hand. Prices for six to eight week classes range from $40–$85. Some private instructors also offer classes at their schools in addition to one-on-one instruction. These usually cost under $100.

You can also board your dog in a school kennel where he is taught the techniques of obedience, house training and proper behavior. This is individualized, private training where, after two to six weeks, you pick up your trained dog. There is usually at least one session with the owner to familiarize him with what his dog has learned while at boarding school. Costs for this type of training are similar to at-home training, plus the added expenses of food and board.

For a state-by-state listing of obedience clubs that will provide you with information on training classes, write Gaines Obedience Lists, Box 1007, Kankakee, IL 60901. Include the name of your state with your request.

You can also contact the National Association of Dog Obedience Instructors, 2286 E. Steel Road, St. Johns, MI 48879 who will refer you to member trainers. Write the Society of North American Dog Trainers, c/o Companion Animal Services, ASPCA, 441 E. 92nd St., New York, NY 10128.

Finally, there are a growing number of animal behaviorists who offer counseling by telephone. They usually have a strong background in animal or human psychology and can determine the causes of problems and how to deal with them by the owner's descriptions of the animal's behavior. Whatever problem you are experiencing with your pet, it may be solvable through a long distance specialist.

Two such specialists are Marge Beebe, (518)393-5244, who has over 20 years experience in pet and pet/family counseling and Ron Berman, (213)376-0620, a dog trainer, behaviorist, lecturer and consultant on canine behavior with more than ten years experience.

Whichever training method you choose, we recommend reading *Mother Knows Best: The Natural Way to Train Your Dog*, by Carol Benjamin. It is an excellent guide that will supplement any training program.

SAVINGS ON PET GROOMING

Nothing is worse than a dirty dog, except perhaps a dirty dog with fleas. Cats, by nature, are self cleaning animals, but even cats get fleas, ticks or occasionally end up in a mud puddle or get caught in a downpour. Professional grooming services can include haircut, flea bath and dip, medicated bath, nail clipping, ear cleaning, teeth cleaning and skin and coat conditioning.

The least expensive way to groom your dog is to do it yourself at home. However, if your dog requires a special haircut or shave, you might want to send him to the groomer between baths. (You can buy professional pet grooming products, such as clippers, trimmers, nail cutters, etc. at a discount through most pet supply catalogs.) If your dog has an especially bad case of fleas, we suggest you invest in a professional flea bath and dip during those times when infestation is at its worst.

Most veterinarians offer bathing and nail clipping. In order to get a professional styling or haircut, you will probably have to go to a full-service groomer and drop your dog off for the day. Recently, mobile groomers, where the groomer comes to your home and provides services from a fully equipped pet salon on wheels, have developed. (In fact, mobile pet services now include the convenience of having a vet come to your home; getting food delivered to your door; having a professional trainer come to you; pet-sitting and taxi services to deliver your pet in style; personalized counseling for your pet; and door-to-door flea elimination service.)

The most unusual dog grooming service we found is the Dogromat (only in Los Angeles, of course) where dog and cat owners bring their pets for a self-service wash. The Dogromat provides you with waist-high tubs, flexi-hoses for rinsing and other accessories to give your pet a great bath (you bring the shampoo). They even do the clean-up for you. Prices for range from $8 to $12 depending on the size of the dog and whether it has long or short hair.

Professional grooming services range from around $15 for small, short haired dogs to $35 for large, long haired dogs. For cats, prices range between $17 and $25. Full service grooming, which includes a shampoo, nail trimming, ear cleaning, flea bath and dip or medicated bath can cost between $35 to $75 depending on the size of the dog.

When checking on prices, ask if there are any discounts or specials being offered. Some groomers will offer from 10 to 20 percent off a full-service grooming or select extra services. A grooming salon in Manhattan, Groomingtail's, offers special rates and services to blind or hearing-impaired people with guide dogs or other assistance dogs.

The organizations below will provide you with information about dog groomers:

☆ National Dog Groomers Association of America, Box 101, Clark, PA 16113, (412)962-2711

☆ Southern California Professional Groomers Association, P.O. Box 143, 1822 1/2 Newport Blvd., Costa Mesa, CA 92621, (714)631-9139.

Be sure to check for local dog grooming organizations in your area as well.

WHAT TO DO IF YOUR PET
GETS LOST OR STOLEN

Just as you should consider health insurance for your pet, you might want to consider one the following, low cost "insurance" services. Unlike collars, these methods for protecting your pet cannot be removed—a major benefit if your pet is likely to get lost or stolen. Any vet who treats the animal later may spot a tattoo or scan for a microchip. So might employees of research facilities where many stolen animals end up.

🐕 Tattoo-A-Pet, 1625 Emmons Ave., Suite 1H, Brooklyn, NY 11235, (718)646-8200 or (800)TATTOOS. Both a non-profit and for-profit group, Tattoo-A-Pet offers pet owners the opportunity to have their dog painlessly tattooed with an identification number that is nationally registered. There are over 3000 veterinarians affiliated with this association and the fee is $20 per pet. Each pet is then given a special tag with the toll-free lost and found hotline telephone number. They also run a non-profit tattoo operation in many shelters across the country. Once an animal is adopted, the adoption agency tattoos the pet. This permanent identification of your pet helps prevent theft and provides a much greater chance of recovery if it is lost.

🐕 National Dog Registry, P.O. Box 116, Woodstock, NY 12498, (914)679-2355 or (800)NDR-DOGS. Founded in 1966, the National Dog Registry is the largest animal recovery agency in the world. By tattooing an identification number on the right hind leg of your pet and then nationally registering the animal with this organization, you can help prevent the theft of your animal and greatly enhance its chance of recovery. The group maintains a 24-hour hotline every day of the year and with over three million animals now registered, they have a recovery rate of over 95 percent. They work with smaller pet identification agencies, such at Tattoo-A-Pet, to help locate animals and their owners. They offer a network of over 5,000 animal welfare officials who engrave the tattoo identification number, usually for just $10. There is a one-time fee of $35 for a member to join the registry. This fee covers the registration of all the animals you have or will have during your lifetime. Not limited to just domestic pets, the agency has registered farm animals and currently has some llamas registered as well as a python.

🐈 Friskies Lost Pet Service, P.O. Box F1713, Young America, MN 55394-1713. This service is tied into an extensive computer system that checks animal shelters, humane societies and rescue facilities within 60 miles of where a pet has been stolen. Membership runs $4.99 plus proof-of-purchase labels (UPC code) from two packages of Friskies Dry Cat Food. Membership kits include a 24-hour toll-free number for immediate pet search assistance, pet protection tips, pet care information, pet information questionnaire, coupons for Friskies products, membership I.D card, a refrigerator magnet with the 800-phone number and a pet I.D. tag with the 800-phone number.

🐈 High technology can also help recover a lost pet. Microchips, injected by a veterinarian, can be read by special scanners. Registered with Infopet, (800)INFO-PET, the chips cost $40 plus $11 per year for each pet.

🐈 If you feel more comfortable using a regular pet tag, Volunteer Services to Animals (VSA) offers FREE identification tags for your pet. Contact them at: VSA (818)764-3773.

WHEN YOUR PET DIES--
PET SUPPORT GROUPS

Losing a special animal can be a very difficult, sensitive time. Although friends and family may be supportive, they may not be able to offer the care and understanding that is needed to get through this period of loss. Children and the elderly, especially, who often depend on pets as a primary source of companionship, may need special counseling. There are pet loss support groups, hotlines and seminars especially created for people who have experienced the death of a pet. Many of them are free and meet at veterinary offices or community centers. The Human-Animal Program of the University of California School of Veterinary Medicine in Irvine, California provides a pet loss support hotline, (916)952-4200. Calls are paid for by the caller. There are no additional charges. The hotline is supported by private donations.

The American Animal Hospital Association has produced a series of tapes for veterinarians, their staff and clients to deal with a pet's death. One tape, *The Loss of Your Pet,* explains the grieving process that often accompanies the death of a pet. For more information contact Marilyn Berquist, CAE, (303)221-4535.

The University of Pennsylvania, (215)898-4529 and Colorado State University, (303)221-4535, also offer bereavement programs.

There are also several excellent books on the subject of loss including:

🐕 *Pet Loss: A Thoughtful Guide for Adults and Children,* by Nieburg and Fischer, Harper & Row, 1982.

🐕 *When Your Pet Dies: How to Cope with Your Feelings,* Quackenbush and Graveline, Simon and Schuster, 1985.

🐕 *Coping with Sorrow & Loss of Your Pet,* Anderson, Peregrine Press.

🐕 *How to Survive the Loss of A Love,* Bloomfield, Bantam Books, 1977.

🐕 *Helping Children to Cope with Separation and Loss,* Jewett, Harvard Common, 1982.

Lifetimes, Mellonie and Ingpen, Bantam Books, 1983.

The Tenth Good Thing About Barney, Viorst, Atheneum, 1975.

When Bad Things Happen To Good People, Kushner, Avon, 1983.

SPECIAL SERVICES FOR FIDO AND FLUFFY

Aside from the "normal" pet services already covered, special discounts on unusual services include:

☆ Pet acupuncture. This treatment helps pets in the same way it helps humans, especially those with arthritis and joint problems. Relief for organic problems has also been successful. Non-invasive treatment administered at acupuncture points on the animal's body has proven effective and long-term in many cases.

☆ Discounts on training for adopted, rescued or neutered pets. As supporters of the movement in pet population control, some trainers give a discount if you acquired your pet through a rescue or adoption service and have had him neutered. Ask local trainers if they offer such a discount.

☆ Free puppy selection service. Before you bring home a new puppy, ask trainers if they will help you choose your new housemate. Professional trainers are very sensitive to the disposition of animals and can guide you in picking a pet or breed that best meets your home situation and needs. Of course, they may want you to use them when you begin your pet's training program.

☆ Animal communication. This unusual type of therapy enlists the ability to receive and send mental images to animals to solve emotional, behavorial and physical problems. Carol

Gurney of Thousand Oaks, California is an animal communicator who, through her workshops (she also offers telephone consultation), teaches owners of all types of pets, from dogs to horses, to understand the language of their animals. She also employs animal bodywork to help locate and relieve chronic pain and other physical problems in animals. Maureen Hall of Sylmar, California has over 30 years experience as an animal trainer, communicator and behavior consultant. She is a certified zookeeper and has trained animals for the movies and theater. Another animal communicator, Penelope Smith, practices in the San Francisco area.

☆ Home delivery of pet food and pet supplies. Several manufacturers will deliver their pet food. Perform, the high performance, premium pet food (for dogs and cats) from the Carnation Company, is available delivered right to your door. You tell them what kind of pet food you want, how much you'd like delivered in each shipment and how often you would like a delivery. For more information call Perform, (800)547-4700, or (800)858-3500 or ask your vet or local pet store about other high quality pet food delivery services.

A new service in our area, Bone Appetit, will deliver a variety of pet supplies to your home, charging prices comparable with local pet stores. Home delivery sometimes may cost a little more, but in many cases, especially for housebound, ill or elderly pet owners, the service they provide greatly outweighs the small delivery charge.

Many pet stores also offer free delivery service, not just on large bulky items (40 lb. bags of food or acquariums), but also fish. These services are normally available *by request* from premium pet centers.

In addition to delivering pet food and supplies, there are also pet "limousine" services that provide emergency transportation, discounts on pet transportation and other benefits. These services are generally provided by boarding kennels and veterinary hospitals from which pets have to be transported when their owners are not available.

☆ Animal training videos. If you have chosen to tackle the job of training your pet yourself, your first thought was probably to find as many books on the subject as are available to familiarize yourself with training techniques. Whether you plan to train a dog, bird, cat or horse, you can easily find dozens of helpful sources written detailing all phases of training of animals. Many are available FREE from the shelves of your local library.

However, as the saying goes, a picture is worth a thousand words. That's where animal training videos are really worth the price. The most effective way for you to attain success in do-it-yourself training is by seeing exactly what you should be doing and what your animal should be doing in response to your commands. Also, by training at home, you can go at your own pace, spending as little or as much time as you and your pet require. Most training videos cost between $17.95 and $49.95. Specialty videos, such as protection training, may cost more. Many contain useful information on nutrition, healthcare, grooming, etc.

Ask your veterinarian or local pet store for recommendations on training videos. Many are advertised in pet magazines and offer free information and catalogs. Animal supply catalogs (see Chapter 7) also offer books and videos. Or write to one of the publishers listed in Chapter 6. Specialty bookstores usually carry videotapes and audio cassettes in addition to books.

☆ FREE veterinary exams. Most veterinarians vehemently support the pet population control movement. Some offer free health evaluations and exams for dogs and cats that have been rescued or adopted from a shelter. Ask if your vet provides this service.

CHAPTER 6

The great pleasure of a dog is that
you may make a fool of yourself with him
and not only will he not scold you, but
he will make a fool of himself, too.

--Samuel Butler

EVERYTHING YOU WANT TO KNOW ABOUT YOUR PET:
FREE PAMPHLETS, MAGAZINES, BOOKS AND NEWSLETTERS

 With very little effort and cost (in fact, usually for FREE) you can find out everything you need to know about living with and caring for your pets. Informative, educational, entertaining booklets and brochures covering every aspect of pet care are readily available for FREE at your local vet's office, pet supply store, kennel club, grooming shop or by sending away for a copy.

Much of the information is provided by pet food manufacturers who hope that once you've read their helpful tips and hints, you will buy their products. Whether you decide to buy their products is up to you; however, you can't beat the price for the amount of knowledge you get in return—it's all for FREE!

The following are examples of some of the hundreds of titles available from the local outlets or by writing away for FREE copies:

From the Ralston Purina Company:

Your Child's Dog
First Aid for Dogs
Is My Dog Sick?
Your Aging Dog
Dogs' Internal Parasites
Your Dog's Teeth
Dogs' External Parasites
Breaking Dogs' Bad Habits
Feeding Your Dog
Puppy Feeding Guide
Dog Feeding Guide
Dog Health Quiz
Caring for Your Dog
Housebreaking Your Puppy and Other Basic Training
Your Child's Cat
Is My Cat Sick?
Cats' External Parasites
Breaking Cats' Bad Habits
Feeding Your Cat
First Aid for Cats
Your Aging Cat
Cats' Internal Parasites
Your Cat's Teeth
Cat Health Quiz
Handbook of Cat Care
Adopting A Pet ...Or Two
Your First Year With Your New Dog
On Being A Good Pet Neighbor

From Hill's Prescription Diet:

Home Care of the Sick Or Injured Pet
Preventive Health Care for Your Cat
Preventive Health Care for Your Dog
Liver Disease
Kidney Disease

Heart Disease
Digestive System Disease
Feline Urologic Syndrome
Canine Bladder Stones
Health Care for the Older Pets
Obesity in Dogs and Cats
Reproduction in the Dog and Cat
Pet Nutrition: Answers to Common Questions

From Science Diet:

The Puppy
The Kitten
Caring for Your Kitten: A Guide to Preventive Health
  Care
(more brochures are available in their FREE health care
nutrition kits)

From Carnation (makers of Perform):

Care & Feeding of Your Dog
Care & Feeding of Your Cat
Care & Feeding of Your Puppy
Care & Feeding of Your Kitten
Digestibility in Your Dog's Diet
Care of Your Aging Cat
FUS and Your Cat's Diet
*Center for Animal Nutrition: Improving the Diet of
  Your Pet*
Training Your Dog
The Traveling Cat and Dog

From Alpo:

Pets on the Go (on traveling with pets)
Puppies, Parents and Kids
Your Dog's Passport to Health
Doctor, What About FUS? (feline urologic syndrome)

*Your Courteous Canine—a Guide to Basic Puppy
Obedience Training*

From Friskies (Write to address below. Enclose 29¢ for postage.
$1 minimum):

*Care & Feeding Your Puppy
Care & Feeding Your Dog
Training Your Dog
Care of the Older Dog
Health Record of My Dog*

From Quaker:

Aggressive Behavior Between Cats (#1050)
Caring for the Older Dog (#1060)
Dealing with your Overactive Dog (#1070)
Dominance in Dogs An Owners Guide" (#1080)
Elimination Behavior Problems in Cats (#1090)
Elimination Behavior Problems in Dogs (#1100)
Fear of Thunder and Other Loud Noises (#1110)
Feeding Your Dog Right (#1120)
First Aid for Dogs (#1130)
Guide to Grooming (#1140)
Handling Your Cat's Aggressive Tendencies (#1150)
Housetraining Puppies and Dogs (#1160)
How to Control Worms in Dogs(1170)
Introducing Your Dog to Your New Baby (#1180)
Is Your Dog Overweight? (#1190)
Strangers and the Family Dog (#1200)
My First Puppy (#1210)
Our Pet's Health Record (#1220)
Pedigree and Health Record (#1230)
The Brood Bitch and Puppies (#1240)
The Dog That Cannot Be Left Alone (#1250)
The Fearful Dog-Easing Its Fright (#1260)
The Vaccination Story (#1270)
Understanding Dog Obedience Competitions (#1280)

Welcoming Your New Puppy (#1290)
What Every Good Dog Should Know (#1300)
Books About the Veterinary Profession (#3050)
Help in the Training of a Herd Dog (#3060)
Single Dog House (#3070)
Some Names to Fit Your Dog (#3080)
Suggested Reading on Dog Care (#3090)
Suggested Reading on Dog Training (#3100)
Suggested Reading on Sporting Dogs (#3110)
Tips on Photographing Your Dog (#3120)

If any of the above pamphlets are not available locally, write to the manufacturers listed below (enclose a self-addressed stamped envelope) for a FREE copy:

Carnation Pet Care Research Center
The Center for Animal Nutrition
5045 Wilshire Blvd.
Los Angeles, CA 90036

Perform (made by Carnation)
P.O. Box 189C
Clearfield, UT 84015

Alpo Pet Center
Box 2187
Lehigh Valley, PA 18001-2187

Friskies Pamphlets
P.O. Box 220A
Pico Rivera, CA 90660

Ralston Purina Co.
Attn: Secretarial Services
Checkerboard Square
St. Louis, MO 63164

Quaker Pet Care Publications
585 Hawthorne Ct.

Galesburg, IL 61401
(request books by title & number; also available from veterinarians)

Hill's Prescription Diet
P.O. Box 148
Topeka, KS 66601

Kal Kan Consumer Advisory Service
3386 E. 44th Street
P.O. Box 58853
Vernon, CA 90058
(write for pamphlets and more information)

Science Diet
(same address as Hill's)
(800)445-5777

Also, write for the titles below for more helpful information about caring for your pets:

🐶 *Puppy Love: Easy Ways to Keep Your Dog Healthy and Happy* has tips on caring for your puppy to keep him healthy. Write to: Heartgard-3's Puppy Love, P.O. Box 931, Whippany, NJ 07981. Enclose a self-addressed stamped envelope.

🐱 *How to Select Your Four Footed Friends* will tell you the things to look for when choosing a family pet. Write to: Pets Are Wonderful Council, 500 N. Michigan Ave., Chicago, IL 60611. Enclosed a self-addressed envelope.

🐱 A brochure all about rabies, its symptoms, diagnosis and treatment is available from the Information Office of the National Institute of Allergy and Infectious Diseases (NIAID), 9000 Rockville Pike, Bldg. 31, Rm. 7A32, National Institute of Health, Bethesda, MD 20205.

😺 Enclose a self-addressed stamped envelope for a FREE copy of the Geisler *Pet Care Book*. Write: Geisler, 3902 Leavenworth, Omaha, NE 68105.

😺 The U.S. Department of the Treasury will send you *Pets, Wildlife & U.S. Customs*. Write for Publication 509, U.S. Customs Service, Washington, DC 20240.

😺 *Traveling With Your Pet* has lots of tips about traveling by car or by air with a pet. Send a self-addressed stamped envelope to: Travel Brochure, American Veterinary Medical Association, 930 North Meacham Road, Shaumburg, IL 60196.

😺 On a similar note, *Vacationing/Moving with Your Pet* is an informative guide available from the Adopt-A-Pet-Foundation of South Nevada, 6423 Sandpiper Way, Las Vegas, NV 89103. Enclose $1 to cover postage and handling.

😺 *Air Travel for Your Dog or Cat,* a list of airlines and their policies, is free from the Air Transport Association of America, 1709 New York Avenue, N.W., Washington, DC 20006.

😺 A free fact sheet, *Transporting Live Animals,* is available from the Consumer Affairs Office, I-25, U.S. Department of Transportation, 400 Seventh Street SW, Washington, DC 20590.

🐶 The American Kennel Club will send you *Guidelines For Disaster Planning*, a booklet that advises dog clubs how to prepare for disasters ranging from oil spills to explosions. The booklet was developed after Hurricane Hugo and the San Francisco earthquake disasters. For your free copy write: Public Affairs Department, AKC, 51 Madison Avenue, New York, NY 10010.

🐶 *What Every Dog Should Know* will help guide you in training your dog. Write to: Gaines Obedience Booklet, P.O. Box 877, Young America, MN 55399.

🐶 Are you feeding your dog too much? Is he getting too little exercise? Send for *Is Your Dog Overweight* from Gaines, P.O. Box 879, Kankakee, IL 60902.

🐶 Would you like to teach your dog to play frisbee? For a free training booklet entitled *Catch a Flying Disc* send one UPC symbol from any size bag of Come 'N Get It dog food with a self-addressed stamped envelope to: P.O. Box 5862, Kalamazoo, MI 49003.

🐱 Receive a FREE brochure on the care and feeding of kittens, entitled *Kitten Care.* Send your name and address along with your kitten's name and birthday to: Young America Corp, P.O. Box A1866, Young America, MN 55394-1866.

🐟 Raising fish is a fun and educational hobby for the whole family. To get started, the Tetra Company, manufacturers of food and books about fish and birds, will send you their *Fish Are Fun* guide. Write to: Tetra, 201 Tabor Road, Morris Plains, NJ 07950.

🐴 Hawthorne Products, Inc., makers of premium equine care products for horses will send you a FREE informative booklet which tells you how to treat common leg and foot ailments in the horse. For a copy call (800)548-5658.

🐱 The Humane Society of the U.S. will send you a list of companies that pledge their products are not tested on animals. They also will send you (enclose $1 for postage) a copy of the *Joint Resolutions for the 1990s* by the American Animal Protection Organizations. For copies of the above send a self-addressed stamped envelope to The HSUS, 2100 L. St., NW, Washington, DC 20037.

🐴 The American Quarter Horse Association, Amarillo, TX 79168 has a FREE booklet entitled, *For You An American Quarter Horse,* for those who are interested in learning more about this breed. Request a copy from the above address.

🐎 The Tennessee Walking Horse Association has a pamphlet, *Tennessee Walking Horse*, that describes this popular pleasure and show horse. Write them at Box 286, Lewisburg, TN 37081.

There are national associations for several other breeds of horses. These groups provide free information about their breeds. Many have their own newsletters or quarterly publications. Some of these include:

🐎 American Morgan Horse Association

🐎 International Andalusian Horse Association

🐎 American Saddlebred Horse Association

🐎 Missouri Fox Trotting Horse Breed Association

🐎 International Icelandic Horse Association

🐎 National Plantation Walking Horse Association

🐎 International Paso Cross Breed Association

🐎 American Mustang Association

🐎 American Paint Horse Association

🐎 American Paso Fino Horse Association

🐎 American Bashkir Curly Registry

🐎 American Hanoverian Society

🐎 American Shetland Pony Club

Consult current issues of horse publications, tack and feed supply stores or Gale's *Encyclopedia of Associations* (in the reference section of the library) for information and addresses of breed-specific organizations you are interested in.

Yet more FREE pet care information from various pet product, drug and medical companies available at pet stores and clinics include:

- 🐱 *A Breakthrough in Nutrition* (Prozyme Products,Ltd.)

- 🐱 *Pet Medical Record* (chart from Pitman-Moore, Inc.)

- 🐱 *Important Papers for Your Cat* (chart from Ralston Purina Company)

- 🐱 *Protect Your Cat Against Rabies* (Fromm Laboratories)

🐶 *Your Dog and the Thryoid Gland* (Daniels Pharmaceuticals, Inc.)

🐱 *Feline Leukemia Virus Infection* (Norden Laboratories)

🐱 *What You Should Know About Infectious Diseases in Cats* (Fromm Laboratories)

🐶 *Protect Your Pet From Bad Breath and Serious Dental Problems* (Addison Biological Laboratory, Inc.)

🐱 *Allergy Relief* (booklet series from The Bramton Company)

🐱 *Home Dental Care* (St. Jon Pet Care Products)

🐶 *How Dog Smart Are You?* (pamphlet about heartworms and hookworms, CIBA-GEIGY Animal Health)

🐱 *Important Facts about Flea & Tick Control* (Farnam Pet Products)

🐱 *A Breakthrough in Nutrition* (Prozyme Products, Inc.)

We also discovered an excellent series of FREE articles published by the Veterinary Practice Publishing Company (Santa Barbara, CA). These booklets are available from veterinarians who request them from the publisher. They consist of a series of detailed fact sheets that are very helpful in explaining the causes and treatment of diseases and medical conditions that may be present in your pet.

Finally, there is a wealth of information available from various animal organizations, associations, Humane Societies and local S.P.C.A. chapters. Write the organizations listed below to request a list of their FREE publications. (Also see Chapter 9.)

☆ American Veterinary Medical Association
930 North Meecham Road
Schaumburg, IL 60196

☆ The American Society for the Prevention of Cruelty
   to Animals
   441 East 92nd Street
   New York, NY 10128

☆ Morris Animal Foundation
   45 Inverness Drive East
   Englewood, CO 80112

☆ The Humane Society of the United States
   2100 L Street, NW
   Washington, DC 20037

☆ Feline and Canine Friends, Inc.
   505 North Bush Street
   Anaheim, CA 92805

☆ Friends of Animals, Inc.
   1 Pine Street
   Neptune, NJ 07753

☆ The American Humane Association
   P.O. Box 1266
   Denver, CO 80201

☆ The American Anti-Vivisection Society
   Suite 204, Noble Plaza
   801 Old York Road
   Henkintown, PA 19064

☆ American Boarding Kennels Association
   4575 Galley Road, Suite 400-A
   Colorado Springs, CO 80915

☆ House Rabbit Society
   1615 Encinal Avenue
   Alameda, CA 94501

☆ Animal Welfare Institute
   P.O. Box 3650
   Washington, DC 20007

☆ The Cat Fancier's Association, Inc.
   1805 Atlantic Avenue
   Manasquan, NJ 08736-1005

☆ Delta Society
   P.O. Box 1080
   Renton, WA 98057
   (800)869-6898 or (206)226-7357

FREE BOOKS, MAGAZINES AND NEWSLETTERS

In addition to pamphlets and brochures, how would you like to begin receiving books, magazines and newsletters in the mail for FREE? Many publishers and manufacturers make special offers to get folks interested in their products and publications and hope you will order more or continue with a paid subscription. Other organizations offer free publications as a public service.

☆ Prof. Berry of the Berry School of Horsemanship will send you a free copy of his 29-page *How to Train and Break* (horses) booklet. Included is information on his special bridle and Western training methods. Write: Dept 2855, Berry School of Horsemanship, Pleasant Hill, OH 45359.

☆ The American Horse Book has a FREE book for training horses (Western, English, tricks and games). Write for *Johnny And The Sheik*, Dept. 36, Covington, PA 16917.

☆ Learn to train like a pro, write: Bud's Bar MB Horse Training School, Rt. 2, Box 506-B, Hereford, AZ 85615, for a FREE 30-page book on breaking bad habits and training colts.

☆ Sunshine Laboratories will send you FREE *Guide to Common Symptoms and Deficiencies in Birds,* a handy reference chart that explains early symptoms of illness and preventive methods. Send a self addressed stamped envelope to: Sunshine Laboratories, 4417 Gentry Ave., Dept. B, North Hollywood, CA 91607.

☆ The makers of Nutri-Start baby bird food would like you to know more about hand-feeding baby birds. For a Free 16-page booklet and product catalog write: Lafebre Company, R.R. #2, Odell, IL 60460. Also, let them know what kind of bird you own and the name of your local pet store.

☆ If your dog or cat gets lost, you can make good use of *Ident-a-Pet,* a free 32-page record book which provides spaces for your pet's medical history, photographs, descriptions and other helpful information to aid you in your search. Send $1.50 for postage and handling to: Pet Books, P.O. Box 2030, Goleta, CA 93118. Mention whether you own a cat or a dog.

☆ *Collie and Shetland Sheepdog* fanciers can receive a free sample of this quarterly magazine (annual subscription is $7). Write: The Cassette, Dept. PHN, 2 Hemlock Cove Rd., RR3, Falmouth, ME 04105.

☆ Young horse lovers can get a FREE trial issue of *Horsepower,* a magazine written especially for them with games, puzzles, handy hints, safety tips and interviews. Write: P.O. Box 670, Aurora, Ontario, Canada L4G 4J9.

☆ If you are a horse lover interested in dressage, combined training, hunter/jumper, fox hunting, combined driving as well as equipment, clothes and gifts, *Midwest Hunter and Sport Horse* magazine will send you FREE subscriptions to their publication. For information call: (219)625-4030 or write: Subscription Dept., 12204 Covington Road, Fort Wayne, IN. 46804. Include information on your particular horse-related sports interests.

☆ Are you a single horse lover? There is a monthly newsletter just for single adults who want to meet others who share their love for horses. For FREE information and a sample copy, write: Single Horselovers Connection, P.O. Box 762, Dept. HP, Elburn, IL 60119 or call (708) 365-2583. Also, horselovers aged 17 and under can inquire about their pen pal service, Junior Horselovers.

☆ If you love watching videotapes about horses, the Video Rider rental club caters to equestrians. They also sell equestrian videos. For free information and a current title list call (800)422-3360 (in Ohio call (800)722-1190).

☆ *The Collins Report* for birds is a monthly report on current topics, trends and recommendations for the health and well-being of the pet bird. For a FREE sample write to: The Collins Report, 26942 Preciados, Mission Viejo, CA 92691.

☆ For cat lovers there's *Feline Follies,* the newsletter for discriminating cats and their humans. This bi-monthly publication contains tales of feline escapades, cat care tips, original cartoons and more. Receive a complementary issue (enclose $1 for postage and handling) by writing to Rainbows, P.O. Box 260408, Plano, TX 75026-0408.

☆ *Perspectives on Cats* is a quarterly newsletter which reports current, unbiased information on behavior, infectious diseases, nutrition, new treatments and vaccines for cats. If you are interested in quality information for quality health care of your cat write: Cornell Feline Health Center, College of Veterinary Medicine, Ithaca, NY 14853-6401, to receive a FREE sample copy.

☆ *Critter Concepts* and *Pet Focus* are magazines edited by a licensed veterinarian, Lowell Ackerman. For a sample copy of both publications send $1 for postage and handling to: P.O. Box 608, Mesa, AZ 85211-0608.

☆ The folks at Friskies publish a magazine entitled *Cat Companion*. The magazine covers health news and information, cat behavior, nutrition and grooming tips, purebred profiles and contains money-saving coupons. For a free sample issue, write: Cat Companion from Friskies, P.O. Box 1347, Elmhurst, IL 60126.

In addition to *Cat Companion* there are dozens of excellent magazines on horses, birds, fish, cats and dogs that will provide you with many hours of entertaining, informative, educational reading. Many publications offer one or more *free* or *sample* issues in a *trial* or *introductory* subscription offer. If you agree to their offer, they will send you current issues (or one or two recent back copies) and will bill you for a regular subscription, not including your samples. However, you are not obligated to continue the subscription or pay them any money if, after receiving the samples, you do not wish to continue. You simply write "cancel" on the invoice and send it back to them. You get to keep the free issues and your only expense is the postage stamp you use to return that first bill. In return, you can have a mailbox full of FREE animal and pet magazines (or any other popular magazine, for that matter).

Nearly every magazine I've ever read has two, three and sometimes as many as four subscription cards inside the pages of copies sold at newstands and retail outlets. It used to annoy me when these little cards fell out of the pages as I was flipping through the articles until I realized that these subscription cards often included a free sample or trial subscription offer. Taking advantage of the publishers' generous offers, I began filling them out and sending them in. Within six weeks my sample issues began arriving. When I received an invoice, if I didn't want to continue with my subscription, I would write "cancel" across it and would not be billed.

Listed below are some of the more popular consumer-oriented pet and animal magazines. You can write them directly for subscription information or buy individual copies at a magazine stand. Many public libraries also subscribe to them and those handy *trial offer* cards are usually still in them.

✮ Fancy Publications, Inc. publish a series of excellent monthly magazines including: *Cat Fancy* ($23.97 a year), *Dog Fancy* ($23.97 a year), *Bird Talk* ($25.97 a year), *Horse Illustrated* ($21.97 a year), *Wildbird* ($23.97 a year) and *Aquarium Fish Magazine* ($23.97 a year). If you would like to receive a sample copy of one of their magazines, write out the following statement and send it to: Fancy Publications, Inc., Trial Offer, Attn: P. Stewart, P.O. Box 6040, Mission Viejo, CA 92690.

> "Please send me an introductory copy of ___(title)___ magazine and at the same time, enter my order for a one-year subscription (11 plus the introductory copy) at $___ (see prices above). If I decide not to continue after examining my first issue, I'll write *cancel* on the invoice and return it within 10 days. The introductory copy is mine to keep in any case."

✮ *American Cage-Bird Magazine*
One Glamore Court
Smithtown, NY 11787

✮ *Cats Magazine*
Subscription Department
P.O. Box 420240
Palm Coast, FL 32142-0240

✮ *Dog World*
Subscription Dept.
29 N. Wacker Drive
Chicago, IL 60606-3203

✮ *Freshwater and Marine Aquarium*
Subscription Dept.
144 W. Sierra Madre Blvd.
P.O. Box 487
Sierra Madre, CA 91024-2435

☆ *Pets Magazine*
  Subscription Dept.
  1300 Don Mills Road
  Don Mills, Ontario M3B 3M8
  CANADA

☆ *Equus*
  Subscription Department
  656 Quince Orchard Road
  Gaithersburg, MD 20878-1409

☆ *Horse & Rider*
  Subscription Department
  P.O. Box 529
  Mt. Morris, IL 61054

☆ *Horse and Horseman*
  P.O. Box HH
  Capistrano Beach, CA 92624

☆ *Horseplay*
  P.O. Box 528
  Mt. Morris, IL 61054

☆ *The Western Horse Magazine*
  321 Kalili Place
  Papa'a, HI 96746

☆ *The Western Horseman*
  P.O. Box 7980
  Colorado Springs, CO 80933-7980

You can often pick up informative and helpful publications at pet shops, feed stores, pet shows and veterinary clinics. These magazines and newspapers are distributed for FREE (or you can subscribe and receive them at home) and are supported by individual advertisers. Below is a sampling of just a few of the publications available in our area. Check your local pet shops for FREE magazines covering animal news in your area:

☆ *The Pet & Horse Exchange* is an all-animal monthly newsletter covering California, portions of Nevada, Arizona, Hawaii and Canada. It is distributed FREE at pet stores, feed stores, pet shows, etc. and includes a wide variety of news, announcements and services regarding pets.

☆ The *Animal Press* is another all-animal publication for Southern California animal lovers. Included are excellent columns, features and news stories along with local advertisements and an animal "Calendar of Events."

☆ *Animal House Magazine* is a monthly newsletter that looks at animal issues and the personal side of interesting people and their work with animals along with a *Pet of the Month* and events calendar.

☆ For interesting news and informative articles about all kinds of pets, pick up a FREE copy of *Pet Care Times* at your local pet store. Articles by well-known authors, veterinarians and other pet authorities make up this publication.

☆ If you want to buy a horse, *Horsemarket* is a monthly West Coast advertising-supported publication that lists dozens of horses for sale as well as a calendar of horse events and other information.

☆ *Today's Horseman* is a glossy, monthly magazine that covers the premier equine news market of Southern California. It's chock full of show information, events, dressage news and features.

☆ Other FREEBIES for our area include *Today's California Horsetrader, The World of Gymkhana* and *Equine Byline*.

We've already mentioned several horse organizations that provide information on specific breeds. In addition, most breed clubs for dogs, cats and birds publish their own newsletter or magazine. Write to the club and ask for a sample issue and subscription information. Contact the following registries and associations for addresses of national and local breed clubs and societies:

☆ American Kennel Club, Library, 51 Madison Ave., New York, NY 10010, (212)696-8350

☆ United Kennel Club, 100 E. Kilgore Rd., Kalamazoo, MI 49001, (616)343-9020

☆ Worldwide Kennel Club, P.O. Box 62, Mt. Vernon, NY 10552

☆ Federation of International Canines, P.O. Box 40, Raritan, NJ 08869, (201)722-6468

☆ The Cat Fanciers' Association, Inc., 1309 Allaire Avenue, Ocean, NJ 07712, (908)528-9797

☆ The American Cat Association, 8101 Katherine Ave., Panorama City, CA 91402, (818)782-6080

☆ The International Cat Association (TICA), P.O. Box 2684, Harlingen, TX 78551, (512)428-8046

☆ The American Cat Fancier's Association, P.O. Box 203, Point Lookout, MO 65726, (417)334-5430

☆ American Cage-Bird Magazine, One Glamore Court, Smithtown, NY 11787, (516)979-7962 (bird societies and clubs are listed monthly in this publication)

☆ American Federation of Aviculture (AFA), P.O. Box 56218, Phoenix, AZ 85079, (602)484-0931

☆ International Aviculturists Society (IAS), 4315 Hwy. 301, Lake Cormorant, MS 38641, (601) 781-9511.

Also, check the current issues of monthly pet magazines. They list national shows, exhibits and meetings.

PET AND ANIMAL BOOK CATALOGS, PUBLISHERS AND BOOKSTORES-- SHOPPING FOR BOOKS BY MAIL

There are literally thousands of books written about animals and pets. There are books about specific breeds of cats, dogs, birds, horses and types of fish. There are wonderful novels and fiction books on pets. There are historical books on the roles animals have played throughout history. There are books for children and adults alike. There are books on the care and feeding of pets. There are medical books and home veterinary handbooks. And, there are hundreds of books on ways to train your pets.

Building and maintaining a collection of books about the pet(s) you love is something you can refer to and enjoy for years to come. These books can grow along with your pet and future pet generations. Today, because of the popularity of pet-related books (and videos), several publishers specialize in publications about cats, dogs, fish, birds and horses. Often, you can find an ample selection from one well-supplied publisher. Most pet supply catalogs also offer a selection of books and videos.

I've always maintained that the easiest way to shop is from the convenience of your home. With mail-order catalogs you don't have to spend hours running around from place to place looking for a special pet product or book. Ordering by mail gives you the choice of ordering from anywhere and anyone in the country, not just those within driving range.

The following are names of book stores, book publishers and catalogs that carry or specialize in animal titles and videos. They will send you a list of names and prices of all books and tapes they stock, for FREE. All you have to do is write and ask for their current catalog. Once you've received their information, you can compare prices (don't forget shipping and handling charges), brands and select from suppliers with the best prices. Often, as a special promotion, they will put a select group of titles on sale and you can save even more off their prices.

☆ ALPINE PUBLICATIONS. P.O. Box 7027, Loveland, CO 80537. Free catalog of dog titles. Specialize in breed books.

☆ ANIMAL HEALTH EXPRESS. 4439 N. Highway Drive., Bldg. 2, Tuscon, AZ 85705-1909. Veterinary care books and animal training and care videos.

☆ AUDUBON PUBLISHING CO. One Glamore Court, Smithtown, NY 11787. Complete range of books about birds and bird breeds. FREE book list.

☆ AVIAN PUBLICATIONS. 3311 W. Country Club Lane, Altoona, WI 54720. Over 200 domestic and imported bird books. Many out-of-print titles. Catalog available by writing.

☆ CARDINAL BOOKS. 306 W. Johnson, Cary, NC 27513. Books for the horse lover's library. FREE brochure.

☆ CANYON CANINE CENTER. 19981 Pleasant Park Rd., Conifer, CO 80433. Large selection of pet books, many below retail prices.

☆ CAROL BUTCHER BOOKS. 3955 New Rd., Youngstown, OH 44515. Out of print dog books (send $1 for catalog).

☆ DENLINGER'S PUBLISHERS, LTD. P.O. Box 76, Fairfax, VA 22030. Extensive catalog of quality breed books, training books and other dog books.

☆ DIRECT BOOK SERVICES. P.O. Box 15357A, Seattle, WA 98115, (800)776-2665. Send for FREE dog book catalog. Thousands of titles on every subject. New and out of print titles. Videos.

☆ DORAL PUBLISHING. P.O. 596, Wilsonville, OR 97070. Publishers of dog books.

☆ E.P. DUTTON. 7 Park Avenue, New York, NY 10016. Publishers of dog books.

☆ EQUINE RESEARCH, Inc. P.O. Box 111460, Carrolton, TX 75011. A complete catalog of books and videos covering care, medical treatment, training, showing, racing and the business of owning horses.

☆ FAZO-CORP PRODUCTS, Inc. FAZO-CORP, P.O. Box 2059, Dorval, Quebec, Canada H9S 3K7. Sellers of cats books. Many titles discounted. Write for catalog.

☆ HOWELL BOOK HOUSE. 866 Third Ave., New York, NY 10022. Specialize in dog breed books.

☆ JEFFERS GENERAL & EQUINE CATALOG. Box 948, West Plains, MO 65775. Good selection of books and videos on care, riding techniques and training of horses.

☆ LEERBURG VIDEO. Rt. 4, Box 231B13, Menomonie, WI 54751, (715)235-6502. Dog training videos. Personal protection, police, basic obedience, puppy training, tracking. Write for a free catalog.

☆ LEWIS BOOKS. P.O. Box 41137, Cincinnati, OH 45241. Large selection of books on the care and raising of fish and birds.

☆ NPA. P.O. Box 527BT, Nesconset, NY 11767. Parrot Lover's Library. Discounts on books and videos on taming, training, breeding, nutrition, health care, building aviaries, etc. FREE catalog.

☆ OWL AND OAK. P.O. Box 222, Groton, NY 13073. Books on cats. FREE catalog.

☆ PM-UNITED. 4545 S. Mingo, HR, Tulsa, OK 74146. Instructional equestrian and related videos. Over 200 titles. Free brochure.

☆ R.C. STEELE. 1989 Transit Way, Brockport, NY 14420-0910. Dog equipment and kennel supply catalog. Discount prices. Hundreds of titles on training, care and breeding of dogs (List #U95-0002). Also carry titles on fish, small animals, birds, horses and cats (List #U95-0008). Most publishers represented. FREE book list catalogs.

☆ ROBIN BLEDSOE, BOOKSELLER. 1640-P Mass. Ave., Cambridge, MA 02138. Hundreds of old, new and imported books on horses. $1 for catalog (refundable).

☆ SILVIO MATTACCHIONE & CO. 1793 Rosebank Rd. N, Pickering, Ontario, Canada L1V 1PS. Canine library from Canadian specialty publisher. Write for book list.

☆ SUNSHINE BOOKS. 1326 Sioux St., Dept. 2, Orange Park, FL 32065. Large selection of books on cats. Covers behavior, health, enjoyment lore, calendars, humor, fiction. Write for catalog.

☆ TETRA PRESS. 201 Tabor Road, Morris Plains, NJ 07950. Complete bird keeper guides written by a world famous aviculture expert. FREE catalog.

☆ THE BOOK STABLE. Dept 5B, 5326 Tomahawk Trail, Fort Wayne, IN 46804, (800) 274-2665. This magazine service offers subscriptions to more than 40 horse magazines, in addition to books and videos. Write for a catalog of all titles.

☆ THE COMPLEAT DOG STORY. 662 Franklin Ave., Ste. 254A, Garden City, NY 11530. Everything in dog books: fiction, non-fiction, new, used, children's, training, breeds, general. FREE list.

☆ THE HORSEMAN'S SOURCE, INC. 8690 Wranglers Way, Colorado Springs, CO 80908. Equestrian video tapes. Huge selection of instructional videos. All areas of equine interest. Free catalog.

☆ THE PET BOOKSHOP. Pampered Parrot Haven, Inc., P.O. Box 507, Oyster Bay, NY 11771. Extensive line of books covering parrots, dogs, cats, reptiles and fish. FREE catalog.

☆ THE PRACTICE RING. Call: (800)553-5319. Exclusively equine titles of horse books for every equine interest: horsecare, keeping, riding, training, children's books, adult fiction, etc. FREE catalog.

☆ T.F.H. PUBLICATIONS, INC. 211 W. Sylvania Ave., Nepture City, NJ, 07753. They publish several series of breed books on dogs.

☆ TOWNSEND PUBLISHING. 12 Greenleaf Dr., Exeter, NH 03833. Books for animal lovers. FREE catalog.

LEARN THE LATEST FROM NEWSLETTERS

Most organizations and associations that support and work for animal rights and causes publish informative monthly or quarterly newsletters. They inform their members of new developments and explain ways in which they can become more involved in these causes. Most pet breed clubs and societies also put out a publication for their members.

There are also the free newsletters we mentioned above which you can pick up from local pet and feed stores, veterinary clinics, pet shows, etc.

Additionally, there are several excellent, informative and entertaining publications published by folks who want to share local or national news information with other pet lovers. Subscription prices vary from FREE to $20 per year. These publications offer a mixture of news, stories, photographs, cartoons, opinions, ideas and items for sale or exchange. These are the newsletters I like to curl up with and read at night.

Listed below are newsletters that have agreed to send our readers FREE (or FREE plus postage and handling) samples issues of their publications:

☆ CAT COLLECTORS
31311 Blair Dr.
Warren, MI 48092

CAT COLLECTORS is an international organization whose members enjoy the common interest or hobby of collecting cat figurines, books, artwork, advertisements, calendars, postcards, collectibles, antiques, paper products, stamps and various other items which bear a cat motif. Their main method of exchanging information is through *Cat Talk* a bimonthly 16-page, fully illustrated newsletter and catalog filled with cat merchandise from new and secondary/antique markets. The newsletter is packed with letters from members, interesting stories tracing the histories of collectibles, personal stories and news about upcoming swaps and trading shows. For a sample package (newsletter, catalog and club information) send $1 to cover postage. For information only on the club, send 29¢ and a self-addressed stamped envelope.

☆ THE PET GAZETTE
1309 North Halifax
Daytona Beach, FL 32118

The Pet Gazette is a charming quarterly newsletter for animal lovers everywhere. It is produced by an amazing 85-year old woman, Faith Senior, who packs her publication with animal rights information and animal/human interest stories. You will love reading the stories and anecdotes sent by readers from all over the world. Now in its sixth year, *The Pet Gazette* is informational, educational and good reading. For a sample copy and subscription information send $1 to cover postage and handling.

☆ PETTPOURRI
5907 Cahill Avenue
Tarzana, CA 91356

Andrea Pett, animal lover and author, publishes this newsletter
FREE to subscribers. *Pettpourri* is filled with trends and issues relevant to pet owners, including food supply outlets (regional),
information on neutering, pet shelter addresses and other helpful tidbits. There is also news and feature stories of interest to
conservationists and animal rights advocates. This is a great
(and cheap) place to find out about the goings on of different
foundations and groups. To begin a subscription, send a self-addressed stamped envelope to Andrea Pett at the above address.

☆ NATIONAL FERRET REVIEW
711 Chautauqua Ct.
Pittsburgh, PA 15214

The Ferret Fanciers Club provides an information exchange
through its bi-monthly newsletter and other informational publications to members. Although ferrets have been around for
many centuries, only recently have they become popular as
household pets. For a sample copy of the newsletter, club information and a literature list, send a self-addressed stamped envelope to the above address.

CHAPTER 7

If I had to choose, I
would rather have birds
than airplanes.

--Charles A. Lindbergh

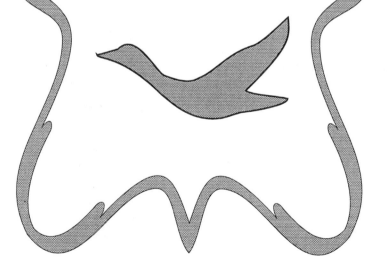

MAIL-ORDER SHOPPING FOR YOUR PETS:

FREE CATALOGS

 As we mentioned in the last chapter, ordering pet supplies through the mail is a convenience that can save both time and money. Shopping by mail is more than just filling out an order form or calling an 800-phone number. If your goal is to shop by mail AND save, be prepared to spend some time comparing prices, selection, shipping and handling costs, sales tax, quality, etc.

I recently bought an orthopedic foam bed with a washable sheepskin cover for my 12-year old English Springer Spaniel through the mail. I knew that this type of bed was going to cost around $50, having seen it at my neighorbood pet store. Since it was a fairly expensive item, I decided it was worthwhile to do some comparison shopping. I called several pet stores in my area that carried the same bed. Their prices ranged from $50 to $75. I also looked through pet supply catalogs and advertisements in pet magazines. I found the exact bed I wanted, on sale, for $35.

However, the catalog required a $50 minimum order. Being the owner of three dogs, I had no trouble finding a couple of other items (also on sale) I needed to fill my order, which came to $52 plus $7.50 shipping and handling. Since the catalog company was out-of-state I did not have to pay sales tax. Here's how my savings added up:

	Catalog Price	Store Price
Dog bed	$35.00	$50.00
Yard Spray	7.00	15.00
Expandable leash	10.00	20.00
Shipping, etc.	7.50	—
Sales Tax (7%)	—	3.50
Total Paid	$59.50	$88.50

I saved $29.00 by ordering the items I needed through a catalog!

Nearly all pet and animal supplies are available through mail-order catalogs. In fact, the incredible selection and choice was surprising. What I like most of all is to be able to do my comparison shopping at my convenience in my home. Also, once I became familiar with my favorite catalogs (which included both discount and regular prices), I could wait until they advertised their semi-annual or quarterly sales and do most of my ordering at one time, with nearly everything being offered on sale or at deeply discounted prices.

The following catalogs represent some of the more popular national companies offering pet supplies. Some specialize in products for one type of pet only, such as birds. Others combine dog supplies with horse products. Many catalogs offer items for animal owners along with supplies for their pets. The final catagory of catalogs are those specializing in gifts, books, clothes, etc. just for animal lovers and owners. These "for humans only" catalogs offer an interesting and delightful array of products, whether or not you own a pet.

GENERAL PET SUPPLIES

ANIMAL CITY WHOLESALE. P.O. Box 2076, La Mesa, CA 92014. Supplies for dogs, cats, birds, horses and fish.

ANIMAIL PET CARE PRODUCTS. P.O. Box 854, Clearfield, UT 84015, (800)255-3723.

MAIL ORDER PET SHOP. (800)366-7387. They carry every major manufacturer of pet supplies. Call for FREE Catalog.

PET WAREHOUSE. (800)443-1160. Bird, fish, cat, dog supply catalog. FREE catalog.

UPCO. P.O. Box 969, St. Joseph, MO 64502, (816) 233-8800. Quality bird, dog, cat and horse supplies. FREE CATALOG. Call or write.

OMAHA VACCINE COMPANY. 3030 L. St., Omaha, NE 68107. Supplies for dogs, cats, other house pets and horses.

WHOLESALE PET USA. Box 9281, Colorado Springs, CO 80932, (800) 444-0404.

FREE VETERINARY SUPPLY CATALOG for dogs, cats and horses. (800)762-7387.

JB WHOLESALE PET SUPPLIES. 289 Wagaraw Ave., Hawthorne, NJ 07506, (800)526-0388 or (800)872-6072.

ANIMAL HEALTH EXPRESS. (800)533-8115. Quality supplies for livestock, farm animals, cats and dogs. Also contains a tack section. Warehouse direct prices. FREE catalog.

BIRD SUPPLY CATALOGS

BROOKDALE PETS. (800)535-8285. Quality bird supplies. FREE Catalog.

DREAMWORK DESIGNS. 4161 Tujunga Ave., Ste. 208, Studio City, CA 91604. Natural hardwood toys, swings and perches for birds. Send SASE for FREE Catalog.

JERICHO ENTERPRISES INC. (800)333-2022. Water dispenser systems for birds. FREE Brochure.

STROMBERG'S CHICKS & GAMEBIRDS. P.O. Box 400, Pine River 69, MN 56474. Aviary sets, books and supplies. Catalog on request.

AVP/ANIMAL VETERINARY PRODUCTS. P.O. Box 1326, Galesburg, IL 61402. Bird product catalog.

BIRD-ON-A-STICK. 1862 W. 81st Ave (U.S. 30), Merrillville, IN 46410. Tropical birds and pet supplies. FREE educational catalog.

BIRDTWEETS. (800)726-8047. Treats for birds. FREE Catalog and price list.

THE FEATHER FARM, INC. 1181 Fourth Ave., Napa, CA 94559. Metal nest boxes for bird breeders. Send SASE for FREE Catalog.

DISCOUNT BIRD SUPPLIES. 20833 1/2 Roscoe Ave., Winnetka, CA 91306. Cages, books, toys, boxes, health products, feed, crocks, etc. Request mail-order catalog.

CLAUSING. Nocatee, Florida 33864, (813)993-2542. FREE bird supply catalog.

LAKE'S MINNESOTA MACAWS, INC. 639 Stryker Ave., St. Paul, MN 55107, (800)634-2473. Maintenance, breeding and baby bird formulas. Write for brochure.

CAGECO. 13081 E. Rosecrans Ave., Santa Fe Springs, CA 90670. Bird cage manufacturers. Send SASE with 50¢ postage for color brochure.

INGLEBROOK FORGES. 151 N. San Dimas Canyon Rd., San Dimas, CA 91773. Bird cage manufacturers. FREE catalog.

MICHAEL'S BIRD PARADISE, INC. 3925 Investment Lane, Riviera Beach, FL 33404. Specializes in exotic birds and U.S.A.-made wrought iron cages. For bird price list and cage brochure send SASE.

ADVANCED AVIAN DESIGNS. 12021 Wilshire Blvd., Ste. #516, Los Angeles, CA 90025. Original creations in outdoor bird gyms, parrot sound-n-shake puzzles, toys, etc. Send for FREE catalog with price list.

SOUTHAVEN BIRDS. 960 Meriwether Road, Pike Road, AL 36064. All types of bird supplies and equipment. FREE catalog.

THE EXOTIC BIRD SPECIALISTS. P.O. Box 268, Robert, LA 70455. Bird supplies, toys, feed. FREE catalog.

DISCOUNT BIRD SUPPLIES. 20833 1/2 Roscoe Blvd, Winnetka, CA 91306. Bird supplies, books, feed, toys, etc. Discount price catalog.

PARROTS TREASURE. 10252 Baltimore, St. Louis, MO 63074. Handcrafted bird toys from all natural materials. FREE catalog.

AVANT-GARDE AVICULTURE. (800)733-4998. Apple diets, bird seeds, vitamins, bird supplements, parrot toys. FREE catalog.

EMERALD BIRD CADDY. 2254 Silhouette, Dept. A, Eugene, OR 97402, (800)343-6253. Bird stands, perches, books and edible toys. FREE color catalog.

LYON ELECTRIC COMPANY. 2765 Main Street, Chula Vista, CA 92011. Bird incubators, brooders, feeders, books. FREE catalog.

PARROT LOVE. Rt. 2, Crofton Dr., Box 253A, Parsonburg, MD 21849. Handcrafted made-to-chew toys for budgies and macaws. Send SASE for FREE catalog.

PARROTS AHOY. 1426 19th Ave., San Francisco, CA 94122. Fun, colorful and safe toys for every bird at reasonable prices. FREE catalog.

T'S EXOTIC. P.O. Box 51, Runnemede, NJ 08078. Grit, vitamins and cuttlebone for cage birds. FREE price list.

EQUINE/HORSE SUPPLY CATALOGS

(Most of these catalogs also have clothing, equipment, boots, personal tack, etc. for horsebackriders).

WESTERN WHOLESALERS. P.O. Box 84, Richardson, TX 75083. FREE saddle and tack catalog.

STATE LINE TACK, INC. P.O. Box 428, Plaistow, NH 03865, (800)228-9208. Discount brand name English and Western riding tack and apparel. FREE disount catalog.

VAPCO. (800)966-5614. Discount horse feed. FREE brochure.

BIG D'S HARNESS. (800)321-2142. Horse supplies. FREE 100-page catalog.

HORSE HEALTH USA. P.O. Box 9101, Canton, OH 44711, (800)321-0235. Horses supplies. FREE catalog.

D.T. INDUSTRIES. Box 460, Exeter, Ontario N0M 1SO, Canada. Horse stall and feeding systems. FREE product brochure.

JEFFERS VET SUPPLY. (800)633-7592. Riding equipment, grooming products, tack room supplies, vaccines, ointments, accessories, etc. (also carries some dog supplies). FREE 128-page catalog.

COUNTRY MANUFACTURING, INC. P.O. Box 10416, Fredericktown, OH 43019. Horse supplies, barn equipment, hay racks, bridle racks, cross ties, lawn and garden.

WIESE VET SUPPLY. (800)869-4373. Horse supplies, vaccines, equipment, etc. FREE 104-page catalog.

STATE LINE TACK INC. (800)228-9208. Horse supplies. FREE 140-page catalog.

SOURCE. (800) 232-2365. Macronutrients for horses. FREE product information.

PARELLI HORSE-MAN-SHIP. (800)642-3335. Natural horse handling equipment and videos. FREE catalog.

RUDL FENCE MFG, INC. (800)526-3297. Quality wood fencing. FREE brochure.

STOCKTON SUPPLY CO. (800)441-5832. Manufacturers of quality wood and wire fencing. FREE brochure.

SUITABILITY. 1355 West 89th St., Cleveland, OH 44102. Riding apparel and horse equipment sewing patterns. FREE catalog.

VETLINE EQUINE. (800)962-4554. Quality veterinary drugs and supplies for horses. FREE catalog.

HEAD HORSE JUMPS. INC. 179-56 Foreston Road, Parkton, MD 21120. Horse jumps. FREE catalog.

BLOODLINE VET SUPPLY. (800) 346-2675. Discount horse supplies. FREE catalog.

ROMER'S. (800)242-1890 outside California, (800)232-1890 in state. Horse and horsebackriders catalog serving ranch and farm needs. FREE catalog.

CATALOGS FOR DOGS AND CATS

FREE brochure on sport collars and leads for the active dog. PROJECT: WAG/PHN8, 2206A Curtis Ave., Redondo Beach, CA 90278.

MASTER ANIMAL CARE. (800)346-0749. Healthcare, training, grooming, fashions, gifts and collectable dog and cat products. FREE catalog.

SCHNAUZER SPECIALTIES UNLIMITED. 625 W. 70th Terrace, Kansas City, MO 64113. Special items for Schnauzer's and their owners. Send SASE for FREE brochure.

CATEGORICALLY. P.O. Box 164, Bahama, NC 27503. Best of everything for cats and cat lovers. FREE catalog.

KITTY COLLAR COLLECTIONS. P.O. Box 970-477, Miami, FL 33197-0477. Handmade original collars for your kitty. FREE information.

DESIGNER DOGGIE DIAPERS. 30100 Town Center Dr., Ste. 0-240, Laguna Niguel, CA 92677. For male dogs only. Want to solve the problem of him lifting his leg all over the house? FREE brochure.

LEONINE PRODUCTS. Box 657, Springfield, VT 05156. Fabulous feline fun furniture. FREE catalog.

PROTECT-A-PET. 734 Lindsay St., Victoria, B.C., Canada V8Z 3E1. Save your dog's life in your car. Custom-made restraint systems to keep your pet in place. FREE information. Send SASE.

KENNEL-AIRE. (800)346-0134. Full line of automobile and collapsible dog crates and pet supplies. FREE catalog.

R.C. STEELE. 15 Turner Drive, Spencerport, NY 14559, (800)872-3773. Wholesale dog equipment and kennel supplies. FREE catalog.

PRO KENNEL SUPPLY. P.O. Box 25226, Little Rock, AK 72221, (800)762-7049. Dog supplies.

CARE-A-LOT. 1617 Diamond Springs Road, Virginia Beach, VA 23455. Dog and cat supplies.

DOG-A-LOG. Central Metal Products., Inc. P.O. Box 396, Windfall, IN 46076. Folding cages and exercise pens.

TRI-TRONICS. 1650 S. Research Loop, P.O. Box 17660, Tuscon, AZ 85731, (800)456-9494. Products for obedience or companion dogs. (The Tritonics system should only be used in conjunction with a proper training program. Please consult with a reputable dog trainer before proceeding.)

WHOLESALE PET SUPPLIES. 289 Wagaraw Road, Hawthorne, NJ 07506. Dog products and equipment.

DOG-MASTER SYSTEMS. 521 Wilshire, Box 1250, Agoura Hills, CA 91301. Puppy and dog training systems.

PEDIGREES. Box 905, Brockport, NY 14420. Pet supplies, gifts, clothing.

PETDOORS U.S.A. 4523 30th St. W., Bradenton, FL 34207, (800)749-9609. Manufacturers of pet doors.

HALE SECURITY PET DOOR. 5622 N. 52nd Ave., #4, Glendale, AZ 85301, (800)888-8914. Pet doors and security pet products.

BETA PRODUCTS, INC. 503 Miltwood Dr., Greensboro, NC 27408. Pet furniture for cats.

CAT-A-LOG. P.O. Box 89, Tylersport, PA 18971. Products for cats.

FELIX. 3623 Fremont Ave. N., Seattle, WA 98103. Quality products for cats. FREE catalog.

SPORTING DOG SPECIALTIES. Box 68, Spencerport, NY 14559. Everything for training a hunting dog.

NEW METHODS. P.O. Box 22605CM, San Francisco, CA 94122, (800)342-PETS. Educated consumer pet products.

THE HERB GARDEN. 417 Pine Drive, Surfside Beach, SC 29575-3237. All natural, environmentally safe flea and tick control products.

NATURAL ANIMAL. P.O. Box 1177, St. Augustine, FL 32085. (800)274-7387. Natural flea control products. Write for FREE catalog.

CATS, CATS, & CATS. P.O. Box 270-FF, Monroe, NY 10950.Write for a FREE 32-page color catalog listing various cat products.

BREEDERS EQUIPMENT CO. P.O. Box 177, Flourtown, PA 19031. Flea control without pesticides. Flea-Master flea comb catches fleas instantly. FREE brochure.

OTHER

INTERNATIONAL LLAMA ASSOCIATION. The Llama Catalog, P.O. Box 37505, Denver, CO 80237. FREE catalog. A complete source of information on breeders, videos and publications, gift items, llama insurance, packers, products and services.

PET LOVERS' CATALOGS

RITA BOOTH STUDIOS. CF8, 732 Pierce, Milton-Freewater, OR 97862. Stationery, rubber stamps, gift items for cat lovers. SAMPLE and FREE catalog.

INCATS. (800)INCATS-0. Original quality Hanes silkscreened T-shirts/sweats. FREE brochure.

GALLERY OF CATS. 1800 S. Robertson Blvd., Bldg 6, #403, Los Angeles, CA 90035-4352. FREE catalog of outstanding cat items by cat loving artists.

REFLECTIONS IN WOOD. 230 Woodland Acres, Council Bluffs, IA 51503. Unique oak framed sayings for cat lovers. FREE catalog.

GABBY TABBY'S TREASURES. 79A Columbia Avenue, Cedarhurse, NY 11516. Cat lover's catalog.

CAT'S EYE. P.O. Box 1088, Kenwood, CA 95452. Note cards featuring unique variety of cat photo cards carrying spay/neuter message. FREE information.

ANIMALITOS. (800)888-3277. Hand-made "Kitty Kat" porcelain earrings with 22K gold accents. FREE catalog.

ART STUDIO WORKSHOPS. 518 Schilling, Dept. 53, Forest Lake, MN 55025. Cards, stationery and gifts for cat lovers made from original artwork. $1 for catalog.

DOG AND CAT PORTRAITURE. 230 West North Avenue, Suite 110, Chicago, IL 60610. Original oil paintings. FREE brochure.

BASILIA. 27 Forest Ave., Lake Grove, NY 11755. Sportswear for dog lovers. Unique, full color designs. FREE color catalog.

LOUJON'S GIFTS. 3322 Hwy. 6 South, Sugar Land, TX 77479. Collectible figurines. Thousands of dog and cat figures. Over 70 breeds. FREE catalog.

STEWART'S. P.O. Box 277F2, Erving, MA 01344. Handcrafted rubber stamps, note cards, collectibles and more for cat lovers. FREE catalog.

DOGS BY THE YARD. P.O. Box 341, Portsmouth, RI 02871. Unique animal design fabrics and novelty items. FREE catalog.

ALL CREATURES GREAT & SMALL. P.O. Box 355, Congers, NY 10920. Specialists in china and porcelain dog figures. Send SASE for catalog.

BANDANDYS. 600 N. Garfield Ave., Janesville, WI 53545. Pet I.D. Bandannas.

THE MAGICAL MENAGERIE. 1348 Commerce Lane, Suite 163-C9, Santa Cruz, CA 95060. Stuffed dogs and puppies.

GALERIE. (800)344-5393. T-shirts, sweatshirts, accessories.

WALNUT MINIATURES. Box 245, Barnegat Light, NJ 08006. Car stickers, decals, iron-ons, T-shirts, sweatshirts, gifts.

CALICO CAT. 330-19th St., #88CM, Oakland, CA 94612. Gifts for cats and cat owners.

CAT COLLECTIBLE CATALOG. 31311 Blair Dr., Warren, MI 48092. Cat art, porcelain cats, plates, dolls, toys, books.

CRITTER PRINTS. P.O. Box 630, Newport, WA 99156-0630. Animal rubber stamps.

FIREFLY STUDIOS. (800)777-9242. Artful exotic birds silkscreened in 6 prismatic colors on T-shirts. FREE flyer.

YOUR HORSE SOURCE. Box 4155HI, Jackson, WY 83001. Breyer model horses, plus jewelry, stationery, sweatshirts, stables for horse minded folks. $1 for 32-page catalog (refundable with order).

BRYER. 34 Owens Drive, Wayne, NJ 07470. FREE color Bryer horse brochure. Send postcard.

EQUINE DESIGN. 5120 Davis Road, Waxhaw, NC 28173. Sportswear, giftwear, stationery and paper goods for horse lovers. FREE catalog.

FILLY FADDLE. 11218 Concho Lane, Houston, TX 77072. Gifts and apparel for horsey people. $1 for color catalog (refundable with order).

THE NEAR HORSE. Box 533HI, 420 Springfield Rd., Somers, CT 06071. Country gifts specializing in the draft horse breeds. T-shirts, sweatshirts, books, brasses, model animals, plaques, tackpins, belt buckles, rubber stamps, jewelry, porcelain horses. $1 for catalog (refundable with order).

WINDSOR HOUSE. Dept. K, 6707 Dogwood Road, Baltimore, MD 21207. Equestrian and Western jewelry and gifts. FREE catalog.

NATURE'S PALETTE SCULPTURES. P.O. Box 691263, San Antonio, TX 78269. Authentic collection of realistic sculptured parrots. FREE brochure.

CHAPTER 8

The better I get to know men,
the more I find myself
loving dogs.

--Charles de Gaulle

STILL MORE WAYS TO SAVE ON YOUR PETS

In addition to the savings I have shown you for products and services for your pets, there are also a number of overlooked and little known sources for bargains and gifts of which many people are unaware.

For example, did you know that there are dozens of contests, competitions and sweepstakes each year that award free products and cash prizes to winning pets and their owners? Pet food manufacturers, especially, run contests to help promote their products. Prizes for winning pets range from collars and grooming supplies to a year's supply of pet food and feature parts in upcoming movies and television shows. Prizes for pet owners include stuffed animals, appliances, vacations and cash awards.

CONTESTS

Here are some examples of recent contests that offered an array of rewards for the winners:

🐈 The WHISKAS Household-Cat-of-the Year competition. Winners in the longhair, shorthair and white categories received an expense paid trip for two to the finals held at Madison Square Garden. The owner of the grand prize winner received a trip to England for two.

🐱 Science Diet Supercat contest for Adopted Cats. All entrants received a bag of Science Diet. Winners in various categories received rosettes and the grand prize winner received a year's supply of Science Diet cat food.

🐱 JONNY CAT Look-A-Like Contest for black and white cats. Winner received $500 and a chance for their cat to appear in a future Jonny Cat ad.

🐶 Friskies Grand Gourmet Sweepstakes. 25 winners each received a one year supply of Grand Gourmet dog food.

🐶 Lucky License Sweepstakes open to dog owners. A match and win game whereby dog owners matched up the first four digits of their dog's license number with the first four digits of the UPC numbers on Jerky Treats, Meaty Bone dog food or Skippy Premium dog food. Winners received a $50 U.S. Savings Bond and were eligible for a $10,000 grand prize.

🐱 Kitty Litter Healthguard Sweepstakes offered a Grand Prize of $15,000 in unmounted sapphires, emeralds and rubies. Instant win first prizes: five unmounted rubies, five unmounted emeralds, five unmounted sapphires. Also awarded: 4,000 instant second prizes of 10 lb. bags of Kitty Litter.

🐱 9-Lives Veterinary Excellence Award. Veterinarians nominated by individuals. The winners were honored for their life-saving contributions. Prizes include a two-month supply of 9-Lives canned samples for their clinics and subscription to *Cat Fancy* magazine. Cat owners submitting winning entries received a one-year supply of 9-Lives canned cat food for their cats and a one-year subscription to *Cat Fancy*.

🐶 RCA "Name that Pup!" contest. Although this was not a contest for family pets, it did involve naming the puppy who accompanies the famous RCA dog, Nipper. The first 2,000 people entering the contest received stuffed versions of Nipper and the pup. The winner received a complete RCA Home Theater system. Runners-up were awarded various RCA products.

🐕 ALPO Petfoods Patriotic Pets Sweepstakes, celebrated the 214th birthday of the U.S. A grand prize of a $50,000 savings bonds was awarded in addition to 62 $500 savings bonds.

🐕 The United States Dog Agility Association (P.O. Box 850955, Richardson, TX 75085-0955, (214)231-9700) sponsors the Pedigree Grand Prix of Dog Agility for dogs of all sizes, purebreds and mixed breeds. Qualifying events take place in 18 regions. Participants must navigate a timed obstacle course that includes weaving through poles, scaling ramps and racing through tunnels. A similar competition is run by the National Committee for Dog Agility, 401 Bluemont Cir., Manhattan, KS 66052.

🐕 You may want to enter your dog in the Detroit-Windsor World Series Obedience tournament, the longest running obedience tournament in existance, held for over 20 years. Working dog-handler teams from all over the U.S. and Canada compete for the honors in novice, open and Top Dog divisions. For information on the next tournament contact: Mira Jilbert, 2789 Pembroke, Birmingham, MI 48009, (313)643-7282.

🐈 Every year the "365 Cats" page-a-day calendar presents the winners of an annual photo contest in their upcoming calendar. Your cat can be a photo celebrity by winning a place in one of the most popular animal calendars.

🐕 *Animal Tales* is a bi-monthly publication that features stories, poetry and artwork about animals. They sponsor various contests for artists and writers for stories and artwork with Thanksgiving, Christmas and New Years themes. Entries need to be about animals and the people who love them. For contest rules write: Animal Tales, 2113 Bethany Home Rd., Phoenix, AZ 85105.

🐕 The Dog Fanciers Club sponsors a yearly contemporary dog art contest. Contact Billie McFadden, 20 Dogwood Dr., Flemington, NJ 08822.

🐕 Come 'N Get It Canine Frisbee Championships are a national contest with judging based on showmanship, agility and difficulty and execution of catches. There is also the Ashley Whippet Invitational which goes all the way up to the international level of competition. For information write Ashley Whippet Invitational, P.O. Box 16279, Encino, CA 91416.

🕊 The Great Bird Give-Away. A $15 tax deductible donation to The Beak and Feather Disease Fund entitled participants to ten chances to win a one of a variety of valuable, exotic birds (one free ticket was given if no donation was made). Among the birds won were two African grey parrots, a yellow nape amazon, a blue Indian ringneck, a blue fronted amazon and a goffin cockatoo.

ATTEND A PET SHOW

Pet shows are one of the most interesting and entertaining events we know of that offer fun for the whole family. Besides the many cat and dog shows sponsored by kennel clubs and pet food manufacturers, there are turtle and tortoise shows, live amphibian and reptile exhibits and numerous bird shows. Recently, several manufacturers and the American Pet Society got together for an enormous show at the Los Angeles County Fairgrounds called America's Family Pet Show, featuring several buildings of exhibits and thousands of birds, cats, dogs, fish, reptiles, turtles, chickens, miniature horses, goats and other small animals.

In addition to the animals on display at these pet shows and expositions, there are demonstrations, product and pet services exhibits and seminars. But what we come for are the free samples and mountains of information that exhibitors give away to attendees. We usually come away from a typical pet show with several shopping bags worth of sample and trial size products, from dog and cat food to vitamins and flea shampoo. Some manufacturers will give as much as 5 and 10 lb. bags of their latest pet food formulas.

You can find out about upcoming shows through announcements in the events or calendar listing of your newspaper. In our area the two largest newspapers, *The Los Angeles Times* and *The Daily News*, both have weekly detailed lists of upcoming events for pets, including club shows, vaccination clinics, obedience classes and "open houses" for adoption. Pet stores also have flyers on upcoming events. Most major pet shows are listed several months in advance in the leading pet magazines (available at libraries and sold in pet stores). Check out the next show coming to your area and start collecting those freebies.

DIAL-A-PET HOTLINE

There are now several "help-hotlines" available for pet owners with questions about a variety of subjects:

☆ Hill's Pet Products has a 12-hour a day toll-free helpline for dog and cat owners with questions about the nutrition and feeding behavior of pets. Call (800)445-5777 to speak with one of their dietary management consultants.

☆ At Phone-A-Vet, (900)988-8877, you can speak with a licensed veterinarian who will advise you on medical or behavioral problems with your pet. Calls cost $3 per minute. For a simple problem this may cost considerably less than a visit to the veterinarian. The service is available seven days a week from 11:00 AM to 7:00 PM.

☆ A similar service, the Pet Lovers Helpline, (900)776-0007, offers expert advice about your pet, 24 hours a day, seven days a week. There are over 300 recorded topics covering pet behavior, exercise and nutrition, first aid, health problems, fleas and parasites and general pet information. The service provides information only with messages from three to five minutes in length. The charge is 97¢ per minute. Call the above number to receive a free copy of the Pet Lover's Helpline Directory.

☆ Cycle Pet Foods sponsors yet another helpline service called Petline. This 900-service offers 24-hour recorded messages by qualified veterinarians on over 300 topics. They also offer a vet resource service, frequent caller program and newsletter. The charge is $1 for the first minute and 50¢ for each additional minute. For a FREE directory of topics contact: PETLINE, 3181 Mission St., Box 9, San Francisco, CA 94110, (800)334-7387.

☆ In the event your dog has been poisoned, there are two hotlines available for help. The National Animal Poison Control Center is administered through the University of Illinois, College of Veterinary Medicine. Callers can either call their toll-free line, (800)548-2423 and pay $25 per case or they can call (900)680-0000 and be charged $2.75/minute for advice. (The charges are necessary to supplement funding of the program.)

☆ A similar service is available through the Univsity of Georgia, College of Veterinary Medicine. The Georgia Animal Poison Information Center provides an animal toxicology hotline service to assist veterinarians in the prevention, diagnosis and treatment of toxicologic problems. The Center maintains a state-of-the-art computerized database that contains information on over 300,000 chemicals and is updated almost daily. Individuals should notify their veterinarians who can call the center at (404)542-6751. They are then directed to a toll-free access number.

TALK TO PET OWNERS VIA YOUR COMPUTER

The CompuServe Pets/Animal Forum is an online computer service where pet owners and professionals from around the world can communicate with each other. Pet lovers can talk, compare notes, give and receive advice and swap stories about their pets.

The Pets/Animal Forum is managed by the Capital Area Humane Society in Columbus, Ohio. The Forum is divided into several sections, each led by a professional in the field to help answer questions and concerns. Sections include: Dogs, Cats, Pet Behavior/Training, Ask-The-Vet, Reptiles/Exotic Animals, Pet Stories and The Pet Loss Support Group.

For more information about CompuServe's rates and other services, including the Pet Forum, call (800)848-8199.

TUNE IN TO FREE PET ADVICE

"Dr. Jim's Animal Clinic," is a nationally-syndicated talk radio program on pet care that takes call-ins on virtually any question you may have about your pet. The show is hosted by Dr. Jim Humphries, a graduate of the famed Texas A&M Veterinary Medical School. "Animal Clinic" airs on Saturday afternoons from 4 PM–6 PM (Central Standard Time) and is broadcast in over 50 markets around the country. The national toll-free number for callers is (800)ITS-TALK. To find out whether the show airs in your area, contact your local talk radio station or call the American Radio Network at (301)532-2563.

CHAPTER 9

I am in favor of animals' rights
as well as human rights.
That is the way of the
whole human being.

--Abraham Lincoln

SUPPORTING ANIMALS:
ORGANIZATIONS AND ASSOCIATIONS

Over the past 15 years pet owners have taken a much more active role in choosing the best health care products and services for their pets. In keeping up with this demand, the pet product marketplace has grown by leaps and bounds, now offering a wide variety of premium pet food and health care products wisely targeted at the growing number of concerned pet owners who want only the very best for their pet.

This increased awareness concerning animal well being is also reflected in the vast number of animal welfare agencies found throughout the world today. As a compassionate pet owner, you probably care about all animals, from stray cats and dogs to orphaned farm animals and endangered wildlife. For this reason you should know that there are more associations and organizations dedicated to providing animals with a better quality of life than ever before.

While government-operated shelters are commonly found throughout the U.S., there are also numerous privately run, non-profit associations concerned with animal welfare. These organizations have varied objectives, but all are dedicated to protecting animal rights by eliminating animal cruelty and exploitation and providing the public with information about animal care and control. A large number of these groups offer shelter for unwanted animals (and many elect not to resort to euthanasia), while others feature low-cost spay and neutering clinics as well as animal care education seminars. Some groups are also quite active in demonstrating against institutions that use animals for medical research. Most groups also publish leaflets, brochures or newsletters that provide valuable animal care data for anyone concerned.

You also might be interested to know that many of these groups rely on a strong volunteer program. If you donate your time at a local agency, you might assist in caring for the animals at the shelter or help abandoned animals find a warm and loving home. Many people find it a rewarding experience to serve in their community. As a pet owner and someone who cares about animals, you may want to contact some of the organizations listed in this chapter for further information.

Humane Society of the United States
2100 L Street, NW
Washington, DC 20037
(202)452-1100

With over 800,000 members nationwide, this group is one of the largest animal welfare organizations in the country. Their overall goal is to prevent cruelty to animals, accomplished through public education, legislative lobbying and taking legal action against irresponsible pet owners, caretakers and breeders. The organization is also opposed to hunting and trapping and the use of animals for medical research. Moreover, they monitor zoos and animal exhibits for any sign of inhumane treatment and strive to protect endangered species and marine mammals. With eight regional groups in the U.S., this group is an ideal source for learning more about responsible pet care, how to reduce animal overpopulation and eliminate animal suffering. By sending them a self-addressed stamped envelope, you can receive a FREE copy of their new brochure, *Just One Litter: Facts About Spaying & Neutering Your Pet.*

International Fund For Animal Welfare
411 Main Street
Yarmouth Port, MA 02675
(508)362-4944

This group is quite well known for working closely with other national and international animal welfare agencies in promoting public education and support concerning the prevention of cruelty to animals, saving endangered species and reducing animal suffering.

American Society For The Prevention of Cruelty to Animals
441 E. 92nd Street
New York, NY 10128
(212)876-7700
(818)985-8686 (West Coast Office)

Founded in 1866, the ASPCA is one of the nation's oldest animal welfare agencies. In protecting and promoting animal rights, they manage hundreds of animal adoption shelters throughout the U.S., offer low cost spay and neutering services, work through legal channels to implement new animal protection laws and provide various public information seminars on the prevention of cruelty to animals as well as the importance of compassionate and humane animal treatment.

Fund For Animals
200 W. 57th Street
New York, NY 10019
(212)246-2096

You may have seen the popular bumper sticker, "We Speak For Those Who Can't," distributed by the Fund For Animals. This group works to protect both wild and domestic animals from cruelty, suffering and endangerment. Their concerns range from saving dolphins exploited by tuna fishermen to seeking more humane treatment of greyhound racing dogs and eliminating medical experiments performed on animals. They often take legal action to protect animals and stage demonstrations to publicize inhumane animal treatment.

Animal Protection Institute Of America

P.O. Box 22505
Sacramento, CA 95882
(916)731-5521

Dedicated to advancing humane animal treatment, this agency produces documentaries, publishes informative newsletters and campaigns for animal rights legislation. Concerned with both wild and domestic animals, they educate the public about such topics as the prevention of pet overpopulation, the unethical use of leg-hold traps, the killing of marine mammals and the decline of endangered species. They also actively demonstrate in protest against inhumane animal treatment institutions. Send them a postcard for a FREE copy of their quarterly newsletter.

National Humane Education Society

15B Catoctin Circle S.E. #207
Leesburg, VA 22075
(703)777-8319

This well-known agency is devoted to fighting animal cruelty and protecting wildlife. Unlike some groups, the National Humane Education Society operates animal care facilities that are dedicated to the permanent care of lost, sick or abandoned animals. They enforce animal rights laws already in place and seek new animal protection laws. Additionally, they promote sterilization of pets to prevent overpopulation, conduct seminars and present films to better educate the public about animal welfare.

Massachusetts Society For The Prevention of Cruelty to Animals
350 South Huntington Ave.
Boston, MA 02130
(617)522-7400

As the second oldest animal welfare agency in the nation, founded in 1868, this group operates three large animal hospitals and eight animal shelters throughout the state. They have a legislative department that monitors animal protection bills and lobbies for animal rights. The organization employs 13 uniformed animal control officers who are responsible for investigating animal cruelty allegations and inspecting animal exhibits and institutions. They also work to inform the public about animal welfare through various educational programs.

Friends Of Animals
P.O. Box 1244
Norwalk, CT 06856
(203)866-5223

The fundamental goal of Friends Of Animals is to educate the public about the danger of pet overpopulation and the need for sterilization. They offer low-cost spay and neutering certificates redeemable at over 1,300 veterinary hospitals across the country. Every year more than 65,000 pets are sterilized through this program. To purchase a discount certificate, call (800)321-PETS. This group operates using a large percentage of volunteers and takes an active stand against unethical animal practices such as leg-hold traps and animal slaughter for consumption or fur apparel.

Associated Humane Societies
124 Evergreen Ave.
Newark, NJ 07114
(201)824-7084

With three different offices in New Jersey, this organization features complete animal care centers with medical services and an adoption program for unwanted animals. They actively pursue animal rights legislation, present educational programs at schools and sponsor various projects as well as run the Popcorn Park Zoo.

Committee For Humane Legislation
1623 Connecticut Ave., NW
Washington, DC 20009
(202)483-8998

Focusing their efforts in the legal arena, this group seeks to pass animal rights laws on both the state and federal level. They are opposed to the use of leg-hold traps and institutionalizing animals for the purpose of experimentation. They are also affiliated with Friends of Animals.

Morris Animal Foundation
45 Inverness Drive, E.
Engelwood, CO 80112
(303)790-2345

As a non-membership organization, this group brings together different animal organizations and individuals concerned with the health problems of domestic and zoo animals. They sponsor medical research studies focusing on assorted health problems and work to improve basic animal health standards. They sponsor a Dog-A-Thon charity program (similar to charity walk-a-thons), hold seminars on animal health care and keep an updated library. Much of their work force is made up of volunteers. To learn more about this organization, drop them a postcard and they'll send you a FREE copy of their *Keep Your Interest In Animals Alive Forever* pamphlet.

Animal Rights Mobilization
P.O. Box 1553
Williamsport, PA 17703
(717)322-3252

A national grass roots organization with a network of more than 100 local groups, this organization works to publicize inhumane treatment of animals, especially cases dealing with large-scale institutionalized abuses of animals. They are active in legal protest demonstrations, legislative campaigns for animal rights and offer educational programs, including a film series, to the public.

The Delta Society
P.O. Box 1080
Renton, WA 98057-1080
(206)226-7357

The focus of this group is to dispense information on the importance of human and animal bonding which can be spiritually, emotionally and physically uplifting. As an information resource center, they help establish guidelines for animal visitation programs to such places as nursing homes, handicap clinics and hospitals. They founded the Pet Partners program in which pet owners take their pets to visit lonely and/or disabled people. All the animals in this program have passed the Good Canine Citizen test which is monitored by American Kennel Club affiliates throughout the country. The test states that the animal has a good disposition and a clean bill of health.

International Society For Animal Rights
421 S. State Street
Clarks Summit, PA 18411
(717)586-2200

This group is primarily concerned with animal exploitation and abuse. They coordinate demonstrations against animal abuse institutions, formulate new laws protecting animals, take up legal issues that address animal rights and sponsor educational conferences.

In Defense Of Animals
816 W. Francisco Blvd.
San Rafael, CA 94901
(415)453-9984

Concerned with inhumane animal treatment, In Defense of Animals is committed to protecting wildlife, promoting non-animal research and taking legal action to assist in animal rights issues. They frequently organize demonstrations at institutions that use animals for research experimentation and attempt to rescue animals exploited in this manner. They also publish a quarterly newsletter on animal rights and maintain an animal abuse hot line.

American Humane Association
63 Inverness Drive. E.
Engelwood, CO 80112
(303)792-9900

As an umbrella organization representing different agencies and individuals, this group strives to educate the public about animal cruelty prevention and basic animal care and training. They work to raise the standard of quality at many shelters and advocate reducing the use of euthanasia by finding better alternatives. Concerned about protecting both wild and domestic animals, they take an active role in lobbying for new animal rights legislation, oversee the treatment of animals used in television and film and provide educational programs. You can receive a FREE brochure detailing their various educational programs by mailing a self-addressed stamped business envelope.

Animal Anti-Vivisection Society
Noble Plaza, Suite 204
801 Old York Road
Jenkintown, PA 19046
(215)887-0816

Founded in 1883, this organization greatly opposes all practices of vivisection (cutting open or operating on live animals, usually under anesthesia, for the purpose of medical experimentation). They publish pamphlets educating the public about animal vivisection and use their funds to sponsor research on vivisection alternatives. They offer several FREE booklets you can receive by sending a postcard. These publications include: *A Guide For Eliminating Pound Seizure; Why We Oppose Vivisection* and a 46-page booklet titled *The Case Book Of Experiments with Living Animals* which details horrifying case histories of how animals are used for medical experimentation.

Activists For Protective Animal Legislation
P.O. Box 10206
Costa Mesa, CA 92627
(714)540-0583

Working with different animal welfare groups and individuals, this organization strives to get anti-cruelty proposals passed into law. They keep a close eye on all pending legislation that deals with animal welfare and often help lawmakers concerned with passing humane animal treatment laws.

Animal Legal Defense Fund
1363 Lincoln Ave. #7
San Rafael, CA 94901
(415) 459-0885

The Animal Legal Defense Fund is made up of attorneys who lend their expertise to animal rights issues. They offer a network referral listing of attorneys throughout the U.S. who will assist animal rights activists and associations seeking legal representation. They maintain a library concerning judical cases relevant to animal welfare issues.

Animal Political Action Committee
P.O. Box 2706
Washington, DC 20013
(301) 270-1057

As a political action group, this organization focuses on supporting legislators who champion animal rights issues. This includes not only domestic animals, but farm life, institutionalized animals and wildlife. They also maintain a list of congressional candidates' voting records on animal rights legislation bills. Relying on a strong volunteer basis, they directly assist in political campaigns and oppose groups that exploit animals. You might want to contact them to find out how you can help support your local legislators who work towards implementing animal rights laws.

American Veterinary Medical Association
930 N. Meacham Road
Schaumburg, IL 60196
(708)605-8070

This association is made up of over 50,000 professional animal health practitioners, including those who work with livestock, lab animals and small domestic animals. They educate the public about important animal health care information through educational programs, films, videos and press releases. They also provide members with insurance programs covering health, life and malpractice. Together with the American Animal Hospital Association, they established the observance of the National Pet Week (each year in May) with the motto "Happiness Is A Healthy Pet."

American Animal Hospital Association
P.O. Box 150899
Denver, CO 80215-0899
(303)279-2500

Members of this organization are all small animal veterinarians from the U.S., Canada and various other countries. The association works to keep its members up to date on medical breakthroughs and on top of management techniques through various educational programs. Members can either be a practitioner affiliate or they can have their clinic critically evaluated

to be certified under the standards established by the association. To educate pet owners, they offer a FREE copy of their
booklet *We Know How Much You Care,* which details the standards you should look for in selecting an animal health facility.
To receive a copy of this booklet or a FREE copy of the circular
Internal Parasites, just send them a self-addressed stamped business envelope.

National Alliance For Animal Legislation
P.O. Box 75116
Washington, DC 20013
(703)684-0654

This lobbyist group works to protect animal rights through legislative action. They are quite active on Capitol Hill and hold
seminars to teach people how the legislative process works and
how it can be used to implement new animal welfare laws.

**National Association For The Advancement Of
Humane Education**
c/o Humane Society of the United States
67 Salem Road
East Haddam, CT 06423
(203)434-8666

Affiliated with the Humane Society of the U.S., this association
focuses on improving humane animal education programs
throughout the nation. They offer educational information,
new materials and guidance for schools, animal welfare groups
and various educational organizations. Professional and regional workshops are also given to help educators instruct the
public about animal welfare treatment. This is another group
that relies on volunteers to implement their programs.

United Humanitarians
P.O. Box 14587
Philadelphia, PA 19115
(215)750-0171

This organization features twelve regional groups concerned with all facets of humane animal treatment. Targeting domestic animal overpopulation problems, however, they primarily focus on the spaying and neutering of pets. If you live near one of their 12 branch facilities and cannot afford to sterilize your pet, they offer FREE sterilization services.

American Fund For Alternative To Animal Research
175 W. 12th Street, Suite 16G
New York, NY 10011
(212)989-8073

This foundation uses publicly-donated funds to offer grants to scientists who are teaching or researching alternatives to using animals in medical research. They also work to have more government funds allocated to exploring humane alternatives in medical science research and attempt to save animals from cruel research treatment.

National Cat Protection Society
P.O. Box 6218
Long Beach, CA 90806
(213)436-3162

Operating a large cat shelter and adoption agency in Long Beach, California, this group takes in kittens as well as adult cats that have been abandoned or are strays. They strive to educate the public about humane cat treatment and practice euthanasia when adoption has failed. Concerned with cat welfare legislation, they publish a quarterly newsletter entitled *Shelter News* which provides the latest animal rights news. For a FREE copy simply send them a postcard.

National Animal Control Association
P.O. Box 1600
Indianola, WA 98342
(206)297-3293

The goal of this organization is to encourage and provide top level training for animal control personnel. Its members include animal shelters, humane societies as well as animal care and control practitioners. They offer audio-visual teaching aides and publish the *National Animal Control Association Training Guide,* a 20-chapter book covering such subjects as animal rights laws, communications, animal behavior and transportation.

Animal Rights Network
456 Monroe Tpke.
Monroe, CT 06468
(203)452-0446

As a non-membership group, the Animal Rights Network works to educate people about animal rights and environmental issues and bring together different animal welfare organizations to provide cohesion among activists. They also stage demonstrations against institutions that exploit animals.

The Cat Fanciers' Association
1805 Atlantic Avenue
P.O. Box 1005
Manasquan, NJ 08736-1005
(908)528-9797

As the world's largest registry of pedigreed cats, CFA has registered over 1,000,000 cats. In addition, the organization promotes the welfare of cats and the improvement of their breed, licenses cat shows held under the rules of the organization and promotes the interest of breeders and exhibitors of cats. The CFA is also affiliated with the Robert H. Winn Foundation, a non-profit corporation which supports health-related studies into feline medical problems.

American Cat Fanciers Association
P.O. Box 203
Point Lookout, MO 65726
(417)334-5430

A service association for the registration of purebred cats and litters, this international group has members from as far away as Australia, Japan and Germany. They sponsor pet shows (including a non-breed household cat show), offer certificates of breeding, assist breeders seeking a better strain of purity and work with clubs that put on cat shows. Send them a postcard and they'll send you a FREE copy of their membership information package which includes an application form.

(Don't forget, Chapter 6 has additional names and addresses of cat, dog and bird registries and clubs.)

Animal Welfare Institute
P.O. Box 3650
Washington, DC 20007
(202)337-2332

Seeking more humane treatment of all animals, this public information organization publishes various books and pamphlets to help educate the public about endangered wildlife, factory farms, lab animal suffering and cruelty, leg-hold traps, the production of animal furs, etc. They also publish handbooks for school teachers concerning small animal health care and endangered species.

Beauty Without Cruelty, U.S.A.
175 W. 12th Street
New York, NY 10011
(212)989-8073

This association is primarily concerned with educating people about clothing and toiletry products that are made at the cost of animal exploitation. They provide consumers with information on products not manufactured at the expense of animal suffering or death as well as products that were not tested on animals. Additionally, they sponsor fashion shows that illustrate alternatives to fur apparel.

Feline And Canine Friends
505 N. Bush Street
Anaheim, CA 92805
(714)635-7975

Focusing their attention on the humane treatment of cats and dogs, this small organization provides education on the prevention of cruelty to animals and promotes spaying and neutering. They offer FREE sterilization services for those who can't afford to pay, operate rescue vans and oppose euthanasia for stray or abandoned animals.

American Horse Council
1700 K St., NW, Suite 300
Washington, DC 20006
(202)296-4031

As a trade association for the horse industry, members include recreational riders, people in the horse industry and those interested in political issues concerning horses. The group lobbies for bills pertaining to equine protection, monitors new tax laws that affect the horse industry and state legislation dealing with zoning changes for horse property. They have five advisory committees which cover such issues as horse shows, health maintenance and horse racing.

American Equine Association
Box 658
Newfoundland, NJ 07435

Members of this group are interested in maintaining a place for the horse in American society. The group also provides public relations assistance to organizations to promote heightened public awareness of equine issues and preservation of pastureland.

American Quarter Horse Association
P.O. Box 200
Amarillo, TX 79168
(806)376-4811

This organization has over 240,000 members consisting of breeders and others interested in the American quarter horse. The group registers pedigrees, maintains records and approves shows, contests and races.

International Association Of Pet Cemeteries
P.O. Box 1346
South Bend, IN 46624
(219)277-1115

The main goal of this association is to educate people about pet burials, including the proper disposal of diseased animals. With 15 state groups, they can provide you with a non-profit guide to cemeteries in your area. Their members include pet cemetery owners and operators and manufactures of pet cemetery products. They work to maintain a high standard for all pet cemeteries and revitalize those that have fallen into decay.

Animal Transportation Association
P.O. Box 797095
Dallas, TX 75379-7095
(214)713-9954

Comprised of companies and individuals who transport animals by air, truck, rail and sea, this international membership organization works to improve the conditions of animal welfare transportation. Most of the members are airlines and freight forwarders, but some breeders also belong. They help regulate the shipment of all types of animals, including domestic, livestock, lab animals and wildlife. For consumers interested in shipping animals, this group offers a resource listing on all their members detailing their animal transportation specialty.

The Pet Food Institute
1101 Connecticut Avenue, NW
Suite 700
Washington, DC 20036
(202)857-1120

The Pet Food Institute was organized in 1958 as the national trade association of dog and cat food manufacturers. Industry-sponsored public affairs and owner education programs encourage responsible dog and cat ownership. The Institute works closely with veterinarians, humane groups and local animal control officials in order to provide information on pet feeding, training and health care. The PFI provides, at minimum or no cost, booklets on pet care and training. They also work with humane associations in developing a model pet ordinance outlining eight steps to ensure proper pet care. In addition to distributing hundreds of articles and broadcast announcements on the importance of proper pet care, breeding control, etc., PFI also sponsors research on the human/animal bond that documents the value of pets to people in our society.

DID YOU KNOW? –
INTERESTING FACTS
ABOUT OUR PETS

☆ Currently, over 55 percent of all American households (52.5 million) have some kind of pet. 31 percent of those have cats, while 37.3 percent have dogs.

☆ Cats outnumber dogs in America 55 million to 52 million. While cat ownership has been increasing dramatically over the last decade, dog ownership has been declining. This is because many cat owners have more than one cat and because more people are living in apartments or condominiums which may allow cats but exclude dogs.

☆ There are approximately 110 million cats and dogs, not to mention all the hamsters, birds, fish, ferrets, and other pets.

☆ One out of every ten U.S. households has a bird; the total number of pet birds is estimated at over 31 million.

☆ Parakeets are the most popular birds, followed by finches, cockateils, canaries, parrots, lovebirds, cockatoos, mynahs, and macaws.

☆ The average bird owner has three birds and has owned birds for over eight years.

☆ 71 percent of dog owners buy gifts for their pets.

☆ House cats live 15 years or longer (45+ years in human years). Occasionally, a cat has been recorded as having lived more than thirty years. Lifespans are expected to lengthen as new breakthroughs are made in nutritional and medical research.

☆ Three out of seven cats in the U.S. are homeless.

☆ 14 percent of U.S. households now own both cats and dogs together.

☆ 23 percent of single people own one or more cats; 17 percent own dogs.

☆ 46 percent of families without children have a cat or dog (33 percent have dogs; 24 percent own cats).

☆ Among families with children ages 6-12, pet ownership jumps to 68 percent (56 percent have at least one dog and 36 percent have one or more cats.)

☆ A cat has 130,000 hairs per square inch on its belly

☆ Persian cats come in more than fifty different colors.

☆ Most dogs sleep eleven hours a day.

☆ Of the 73 percent of owners who let their dog sleep in the bedroom, 33 percent allow them in bed.

☆ 67 percent of dog owners have a picture of them in their wallets.

☆ 40 percent of dog owners celebrate their pet's birthday every year.

☆ 69 percent of dog owners talk to them as if they were people.

☆ Cocker spaniels are ranked the highest in breed popularity (according to the American Kennel Club, 1990 ranking). They are followed by, in order of rank, Labrador Retrievers, Poodles, Golden Retrievers, Rottweilers, German Shepherds, Chow Chows, Dachshunds, Beagles and Miniature Schnauzers.

☆ Persian cats are the most popular purebred cat breed (according to the Cat Fanciers' Association, 1990 ranking). Others in order of rank are: Siamese, Maine coon cats, Abyssinians, exotic shorthairs, oriental shorthairs, Scottish folds, Burmese, American shorthairs and Birmans.

Additional *More-for-Your-Money Guides* Available from Probus Publishing

Free Food . . . and More, Linda Bowman, Order #220, $9.95

How to Go to College for Free, Linda Bowman, Order #219, $9.95

How to Fly for Free, Linda Bowman, Order #217, $9.95

Freebies (and More) for Folks Over 50, Linda Bowman, Order #218, $9.95

Freebies for Kids and Parents, Too, Linda Bowman, Order #278, $9.95

Please use order form on next page

ORDER FORM

Quantity	Title	Price

Payment: MasterCard/Visa/American Express accepted. When ordering by credit card your account will not be billed until the book is shipped. You may also reserve your order by phone or by mailing this order form. When ordering by check or money order, you will be invoiced upon publication. Upon receipt of your payment, the book will be shipped. Please add $3.50 for postage and handling for the first book and $1.00 for each additional copy.

Subtotal _____

IL residents add 7% tax _____

Shipping and Handling _____

Total _____

Credit Card # _____

Expiration Date _____

Name _____

Address _____

City, State, Zip _____

Telephone _____

Signature _____

Mail Orders to:

PROBUS PUBLISHING COMPANY
1925 N. Clybourn Avenue
Chicago, IL 60614

or Call:

1-800 PROBUS-1

B11

About the Author

Linda Bowman is a professional bargain hunter. As a mother and career woman with two children and a husband, she found that even a two-income family has trouble meeting necessary expenses. In these uncertain economic times it is difficult enough just to take care of one's responsibilities, let alone find the extra cash to enjoy life. Through her own experiences, Linda Bowman has found infinite sources for free things—from air travel to college education and pet supplies to meals. Her friends and family encouraged her to share these experiences and so she began the newsletter "The Best Things in Life for Free." Subsequently, Bowman put together six books with the best information on the subjects she could collect: *How to Fly for Free, How to Go to College for Free, Freebies and More for Folks Over 50, Free Food and More, Free Stuff for Your Pets,* and *Freebies for Kids and Parents, Too!* She has been on nationally syndicated radio and television.